REVELATION EXPLAINED

GOD'S BLESSINGS AND WRATH

LESLIE M. JOHN

REVELATION EXPLAINED

GOD'S BLESSINGS AND WRATH

LESLIE M. JOHN

The entire text of this book and graphics are deposited with Library of Congress Copyright Office, 101 Independence Avenue, SE Washington, DC 20559-6000, USA. This work is protected by Law in US; and internationally, according to The Berne Convention 1971

ISBN-10:0990780163

ISBN-13:978-0-9907801-6-8

PREFACE

My mission is to proclaim the good news of our Lord Jesus Christ as revealed to me through Holy Bible and from various teachers, preachers, and commentators. This is my voluntary service to God in the name of His only begotten Son Lord Jesus Christ.

I share the truth of knowledge of God with others with good intention of bringing them to the knowledge of the living God, the God of Abraham, the God of Isaac, the God of Jacob, and the Father of our Lord Jesus Christ. My mission is to proclaim the Gospel of Lord Jesus Christ and not converting forcibly anyone to Christianity.

There are fundamental Christian doctrines that I believe in and I will not compromise on those doctrines. They are:

God is Triune: The Father, The Son and The Holy Spirit. They are not three Gods, but One God in three persons, co-equal-co-existent and functionally different.

There is no salvation except by Grace through Faith in Lord Jesus Christ. I believe in:

"That if thou shalt confess with thy mouth the Lord Jesus, and shalt believe in thine heart that God hath raised him from the dead, thou shalt be saved" (Romans 10:9)

One may accept or reject any or part of my writings/teachings. No offense is meant to any individual or any religion or any organization. Please visit http://www.lesliejohn.net/

I pray for the peace of Jerusalem and desire that all Jews may accept Lord Jesus as their personal Savior and Messiah.

"Pray for the peace of Jerusalem: they shall prosper that love thee" (Psalms 122:6)

I firmly believe in the saying of Jesus, who said:

"No man can come to me, except the Father which hath sent me draw him: and I will raise him up at the last day" John 6:44.

My efforts to teach or preach are of no use unless Lord Jesus Christ Himself intervenes and the Father draws a person unto Him.

All Scriptures in electronic format are from King James Version (KJV) from Open domain, and

English Standard Version (ESV)

The Holy Bible, English Standard Version Copyright © 2001 by Crossway Bibles, a division of Good News Publishers

Description:

The Book of Revelation is the only book in the Bible which says "Blessed is the one who reads aloud the words of this prophecy, and blessed are those who hear, and who keep what is written in it, for the time is near" (Revelation 1:3 ESV)

Many people are afraid of reading, writing and to expound the Book of Revelation because of the warning which reads...

"I warn everyone who hears the words of the prophecy of this book: if anyone adds to them, God will add to him the plagues described in this book, and if anyone takes away from the words of the book of this prophecy, God will take away his share in the tree of life and in the holy city, which are described in this book" (Revelation 22:18-19 ESV)

Sure enough if we add or remove any word written in the Book of Revelation "God will take away his share in the tree of life and in the holy city, which are described in this book" but there is nothing wrong to expound what is in it to the best of our knowledge in order to understand better and to teach others.

As I wrote this book I learnt more about the prophecies contained in this book, and I hope the reader will be blessed by understanding the Book of Revelation and help others understand.

The Book of Revelation deals with Lord Jesus Christ's second coming, the seven letters to the Seven Churches, God's wrath on those who reject Lord Jesus Christ as their Messiah, the defeat of Satan, and His abundant blessings on those who believe in Him and accept Jesus as the Lord.

Contents

REVELATION CHAPTER 1 – AN EXPOSITION

PROLOGUE

In the prologue of Revelation we are given information as to who revealed the things that should come to pass soon. It is the revelation or unveiling of the things by the Son, according to the will of the Father, to His servants and the message was sent by the Lord through His angel, who revealed those things to His servant John, who bore witness to the word of God, and to the testimony of Jesus Christ, and to the things that he saw (cf. Rev.1:1). His testimony was similar to his assertion in 1 John 1:1-3 where he wrote that the fellow-disciples of Jesus Christ and he declared those things that they saw and heard in order that the readers and listeners may have fellowship with them, and also with the Father, and with His Son Jesus Christ (cf. 1 John 1:1-3)

BLESSINGS

Revelation is the only book which says blessed are those who read aloud the words of that book; and those who hear and who keep what is written in it because the time is near. (As I expound the book of Revelation, I pray that I may not replace or add any word in the book; and this exposition is nothing but an explanation of the text as I understand. It is imperative that every reader should read the text as it is in the book of Revelation and be guided by the Holy Spirit to understand it. I obey the Lord and take serious warning mentioned in

Revelation 22:18. I suggest, therefore, that every reader should also take note of the said serious warning).

WARNING

"I warn everyone who hears the words of the prophecy of this book: if anyone adds to them, God will add to him the plagues described in this book, and if anyone takes away from the words of the book of this prophecy, God will take away his share in the tree of life and in the holy city, which are described in this book" (Revelation 22:18-19 ESV)

JOHN'S WISHES

John wishes Grace and Peace, to the seven churches in Asia, from the LORD who is, and who was, and who is to come, as also from the seven spirits who are before His throne and from Lord Jesus Christ the faithful witness, the firstborn of the dead and the ruler of kings on earth. The LORD is eternal and so is His name. When Moses asked the LORD as to what His name was, the LORD declared "I AM THAT I AM".

"And God said unto Moses, I AM THAT I AM: and he said, Thus shalt thou say unto the children of Israel, I AM hath sent me unto you" (Exodus 3:14)

Seven is the number of fullness in the Scriptures, and, therefore, the words "seven spirits" is the reference to the Holy Spirit.

John worships the Lord by asserting that the Lord loved us and freed us from our sins by His blood and made us kingdom, priests to the Father, and therefore, he renders to Him glory and dominion for ever and ever. One thing that is worthy to take note of is that when Lord Jesus Christ comes with the clouds every eye will see him. Everyone, even those who pierced Him and all tribes of the earth will remember their treatment of the Lord, and wail. John wishes that it may even be so. Amen.

Lord Jesus Christ says "I am the Alpha and the Omega, who is and who was and who is to come, the Almighty"

JOHN'S VISION

The Lord gave John privilege to see vision, while he was on the island called Patmos, in order that he may bear the testimony of Jesus Christ. He was in the Spirit on the Lord's Day, which was the day of resurrection of Lord Jesus Christ and it is the first day of the week. He heard behind him a loud voice like a trumpet saying, "Write what you see in a book and send it to the seven churches, to Ephesus and to Smyrna and to Pergamum and to Thyatira and to Sardis and to Philadelphia and to Laodicea."

THE LORD AS HE IS

When John heard the sound he turned he heard the voice of the Lord speaking to him. He saw seven golden lampstands, and in the midst of the lampstands one like a son of man, clothed with a long robe and with a golden sash (scarf) around his chest. The hairs of his head were white, like white wool, like snow. His eyes were like a flame of fire, His feet were like burnished bronze, refined in a furnace, and His voice was like the roar of many waters. In His right hand he held seven stars, from His mouth came a sharp two-edged sword, and His face was like the sun shining in full strength.

When John saw Him, he fell at His feet as though he were dead. But the Lord laid His hands on John and said...

FEAR NOT

The Lord said to John not to be afraid of anything because He is the first and the last and the living One. He died, and is alive forevermore. He has the keys of the place where the souls of the dead remain and the bottomless pit. He had been there and came alive and, therefore, we who are the children of God need not be afraid of death because we will also rise from the dead. The Lord commanded him to write the things that he has seen in the vision (that is of the things narrated in Chapter 1), and of those things that were in his days (that is the state of the seven churches during his days), and of those things that are to take place in future (that is of those things that would take place as narrated from Chapters 4 to 22). The Lord revealed the mystery to him that the seven stars he saw are the seven angels (that is seven messengers) of the seven churches, and the seven lampstands are the seven churches. (cf. Rev. 1:17b-20)

CHAPTER 2
TO THE SEVEN CHURCHES

INTRODUCTION

"Nevertheless I have somewhat against thee, because thou hast left thy first love" (Revelation 2:4)

At the end of Revelation Chapter 1 Lord Jesus Christ revealed to John that the seven stars in His hands were seven angels (i.e. the messengers) and the seven candlesticks were seven churches. He walks in the midst of them and constantly watches over them. The Lord desired to send out His message to these churches; firstly to individual churches and then to all the churches. The churches mentioned in chapter 1:19 are the churches which were in Asia Minor. The letters containing the message of the Lord was sent out by John to these churches. The letters were literal and the churches were literal; none of them were allegorical or symbolical. They were the churches at: (1) Ephesus, (2) Smyrna, (3) Pergamum, (4) Thyatira, (5) Sardis, (6) Philadelphia, and (7) Laodicea

The letters were circulated to each individual church first and then to all the seven churches in sequence in Asia Minor. The messenger of each church, who was either a pastor or elder, read out the contents of the letter in the church and then passed it on to the next church. Thus these letters containing messages of the Lord were not only dealing with contemporary issues but were prophetical to deal with future churches.

To most of those seven churches the messages contained initial appreciation; then their fallen status and lastly the warning that they should repent and improve upon their condition. However, the Lord was full of appreciation of the church in Philadelphia and full of condemning words of the church in Laodicea. Philadelphia church was known to have existed historically during 1800 AD when Christian movement progressed vigorously. The church in Laodicea was people's church and the people ruled the church and, therefore, they had many issues within and without.

The messages of the Lord were not only applicable to all the then churches but they are applicable to us in the present days as well. They contain the real concerns of our Lord Jesus Christ.

"And he had in his right hand seven stars: and out of his mouth went a sharp two-edged sword: and his countenance was as the sun shineth in his strength" (Revelation 1:16)

CHAPTER 3
TO THE CHURCH IN EPHESUS

(From Revelation Chapter 2)

Apostle Paul wrote to the church in Ephesus in about AD 62 and John wrote in about 96 AD (i.e. after about 34 years). When Paul wrote to the church in Ephesus he was full of praise and wrote of their blessings in heaven. He wrote: "Blessed be the God and Father of our Lord Jesus Christ, who hath blessed us with all spiritual blessings in heavenly places in Christ" (Ephesians 1:3) and as he came to 6th Chapter he warned them to put on whole armor of God that they may be able to stand against the wiles of the devil.

"Put on the whole armour of God, that ye may be able to stand against the wiles of the devil" (Ephesians 6:11)

THE RIGHT DOCTRINES

"Beloved, believe not every spirit, but try the spirits whether they are of God: because many false prophets are gone out into the world. Hereby know ye the Spirit of God: Every spirit that confesseth that Jesus Christ is come in the flesh is of God: And every spirit that confesseth not that Jesus Christ is come in the flesh is not of God: and this is that spirit of antichrist, whereof ye have heard that it should come; and even now already is it in the world" (1 John 4:1-3)

The letter to Ephesus from John indicates that they have slowly but surely fallen down from their earlier stand and ardent love for the Lord. The Lord was pleased of the works of Ephesus that they showed great love towards Him by accepting into their church the preachers, who preached the right doctrines, while rejecting the false doctrines. They tested the spirits and according as John wrote in his 4th epistle.

"I know thy works, and thy labour, and thy patience, and how thou canst not bear them which are evil: and thou hast tried them which say they are apostles, and are not, and hast found them liars" (Revelation 2:2)

The Lord appreciated them for hating Nicolaitans and their doctrines.

"But this thou hast, that thou hatest the deeds of the Nicolaitans, which I also hate" (Revelation 2:6)

THE WARNING

The epistles of John namely, 1st John, 2nd John, 3rd John, and of Jude all contained warnings as to how not to entertain false preachers but entertain preachers who confess that Lord Jesus Christ came in the flesh and dwelt among us.

This was the major concern in all the early churches after Jesus ascended into heaven and entrusted the work of building His church. The Lord was not only talking as to how they loved Him but He was conveying His deep concern as to how they drifted away from their first love and from their firm stand. They initially accepted and proclaimed the right doctrines but have slowly become lenient to them.

The Lord warned them to keep false teachers away from among them and repent of their works; lest He would remove their lampstand from them. The Lord's warning as we see in Scriptures is not for casting his children into 'lake of fire' but to save from it. The Lord chastens his children in order that they may come back to Him from their backslidden position.

"He that hath an ear, let him hear what the Spirit saith unto the churches; To him that overcometh will I give to eat of the tree of life, which is in the midst of the paradise of God" (cf. Ezekiel 28:13; 31:8)

THE CHASTENING

The Lord's chastening is not to be despised. He will not cast us away from his fold but he desires to correct us of our failures with severe warnings and chastening. Consider the endurance of God, His patience and longsuffering with sinners. Let us not be wearied or faint but trust in the Lord that all thing work for good for those who believe in Him.

"For consider him that endured such contradiction of sinners against himself, lest ye be wearied and faint in your minds" (Hebrews 12:3)

"And ye have forgotten the exhortation which speaketh unto you as unto children, My son, despise not thou the chastening of the Lord, nor faint when thou art rebuked of him" (Hebrews 12:5)

CHAPTER 4
TO THE CHURCH IN SMYRNA

(From Revelation Chapter 2)

"He that hath an ear, let him hear what the Spirit saith unto the churches; He that overcometh shall not be hurt of the second death" (Revelation 2:11)

The seven letters sent to seven churches in Asia Minor were literal letters in different periods of time of church history. After first letter was written to the church in Ephesus, John writes second letter to the church in Smyrna according to the will of Lord Jesus Christ.

Smyrna was a city on the west coast of Asia Minor and the modern city is known as "Ismir" in Turkey. Christians in this city suffered persecution and stood for the Lord. God, who is eternal, knew their works, sufferings, and poverty but He calls them rich because they stood for the Lord. They will have their rewards in due time.

The Pharisees, scribes and Sadducees were the main sects whom Lord Jesus had to confront during His earthly ministry. The Pharisees called themselves as the descendants from Abraham and therefore, they claimed to be the Jews. Jesus confronted them by saying that He, who is the Son of God, was with the Father, even before Abraham was born. Then they took up stones to throw at Jesus but He went out of the temple going through the midst of them and they could not do any harm to Him (cf. John 8:59)

These Pharisees, who claimed as Jews because they were the sons of Abraham, did not realize that Abraham was a Gentile and he was from "Ur" of the "Chaldees". He believed in God and His faith was counted as righteousness for him. Isaac was the promised son of Abraham and Jacob was the chosen son of Isaac and Jacob was called "Israel". The tribe of Judah, and Benjamin were collectively called the "Jews". Some Levites, who assimilated into Southern Kingdom of Israel, have the blessings to be called as "Jews". The Lord calls all those who call themselves as "Jews" and are not Jews as "Synagogue of Satan". Synagogues were the places of worship for Jews. Jesus taught in Synagogues, and likewise Paul went first to Synagogues to preach the Gospel to Jews and then to Gentiles.

"Your father Abraham rejoiced to see my day: and he saw it, and was glad. Then said the Jews unto him, Thou art not yet fifty years old, and hast thou seen Abraham? Jesus said unto them, Verily, verily, I say unto you, Before Abraham was, I am" (John 8:56-58)

Lord Jesus came down heavily upon Pharisees and Scribes and said:

"Ye are of your father the devil, and the lusts of your father ye will do. He was a murderer from the beginning, and abode not in the truth, because there is no truth in him. When he speaketh a lie, he speaketh of his own: for he is a liar, and the father of it" (John 8:44)

The Lord encourages Christians at Smyrna not to be afraid of anyone, who persecute them or kill them because they can only harm the physical body and not the soul. This assurance from the Lord is applicable to us also. Fear the Lord who has the authority over your soul. Authorities, who are controlled by the devil, may throw the believers into prison for standing for the Lord, but it would be for a very short period as ten days. Short period is usually referred to as 'ten days' in scriptures.

"And her brother and her mother said, Let the damsel abide with us a few days, at the least ten; after that she shall go" (Genesis 24:55)

"And it came to pass about ten days after, that the LORD smote Nabal, that he died" (1 Samuel 25:38)

The Lord encourages that they should be faithful unto death and if they remain faithful until the end He will give a 'crown of life'. He that overcomes

Everyone will have to die once on this earth. However there are some exceptions like Enoch and Elijah who were taken up alive into heaven and those believers, who will be caught up into heaven when "the Lord himself shall descend from heaven with a shout, with the voice of the archangel, and with the trump of God" when "the dead in Christ shall rise first" and then the believers who are alive and remain "shall be caught up together with them in the clouds, to meet the Lord in the air" to be with the Lord for ever (cf. 1 Thessalonians 4:16-17)

"Blessed and holy is he that hath part in the first resurrection: on such the second death hath no power, but they shall be priests of God and of Christ, and shall reign with him a thousand years" (Revelation 20:6)

Blessed are those who have part in the first resurrection. There will be a general resurrection of all unbelievers at the end who rise only to face judgment before the "great white throne". All those who are judged at the "great white throne" will be cast into "lake of fire" and that is the second death. The Lord saves all the children of God from suffering the second death which is to be cast into "lake of fire".

"And death and hell were cast into the lake of fire. This is the second death". (Revelation 20:14)

"But the fearful, and unbelieving, and the abominable, and murderers, and whoremongers, and sorcerers, and idolaters, and all liars, shall have their part in the lake which burneth with fire and brimstone: which is the second death" (Revelation 21:8)

Repent and be saved of the "second death". Confess Jesus is the Lord and believe in heart that God raised him from death.

CHPTER 5
TO THE CHURCH IN PERGAMUM

(From Revelation Chapter 2)

"But I have a few things against thee, because thou hast there them that hold the doctrine of Balaam, who taught Balac to cast a stumblingblock before the children of Israel, to eat things sacrificed unto idols, and to commit fornication" (Revelation 2:14)

Letter to the Church at Pergamum is the third letter of the seven literal letters to the seven churches in Asia Minor written by John at the instructions of Lord Jesus Christ. Pergamum was a city where the idolatry was at its peak with beautiful temples to the four gods namely "Zeus", "Dionysus", "Athena" and "Asklepios".

Lord Jesus Christ called this city as the place "where Satan's throne is". The Gospel of Jesus Christ reached very quickly to this city where a God's servant namely "Antipas" was martyred. In the early days of Christianity the disciples of Jesus Christ and His followers, such as Stephen and Antipas, were martyred. Although Bible does not say much about "Antipas" yet it is known from the history that he could have been a pastor or elder of the church there.

Lord Jesus Christ appreciated the works of the church in Pergamum. He acknowledged that they stood firm in the midst of oppressors and tribulations, such as the one by name Antipas, His faithful witness, was martyred for His name's sake at this city. The believers at this city held fast to the Lord and did not deny His name in spite of being in the midst of trials and tribulations.

Lord Jesus Christ has sharp two-edge sword in His mouth and he said He will deal severely with those who persecute the children of God. His countenance is of sun that shines in his strength. The Lord said He will come quickly and blessed is the one who keeps the prophecy of the book of Revelation. When the wicked is revealed, the Lord will consume him with the spirit of his mouth and shall destroy with the brightness of his coming (cf. Revelation 22:7; 2 Thessalonians 2:8)

The Lord sent out to the church in Pergamum His message, which was also prophetical to all churches in the present age that idolatry, sexual immorality, introduction of any kind of other mediatorship than His mediatorship will not be tolerated.

Even as Jesus appreciated the works of the church in Pergamum, He says to them that He has something against them and that they should repent and improve upon their condition. They had within their church two categories of people; one that followed the doctrine of Balaam and another that followed Nicolatains.

THE DOCTRINE OF BALAAM

Balaam the son of Beor was a seer from a city called Pathor in Mesapotamia. He had the gift of prophecy (cf. Numbers 22:2 through Numbers 24:25; Num. 31:8, 16; Deut. 23:4; Joshua 13:22; 24:9; Nehemiah 13:2; Micah 6:5; 2 Peter 2:15; Jude 1:11; Revelation 2:14.). He taught Balak to cast a stumbling block before the children of Israel to eat the things sacrificed to idols and to commit fornication (Rev.2:14-15)

When the children of Israel pitched their tents in the plains of Moab Balaam went at the instigation of Balak to curse the children of Israel expecting huge wealth in reward. However, when God controlled the mouth of Balaam he showered blessings upon Israel instead of curses.

THE DOCTRINE OF NICOLAITANS

Nicolaitans doctrine was almost similar to that of the doctrine of Balaam. The doctrine of Nicolaitans came from Nicolas who taught that there is a division between clergy and the laity (i.e. the overseers in the Church and the congregation). They not only cast stumbling block before the congregation that they should strictly refuse to eat the things offered to idols but they also taught that Pastors or Bishops are mediators between God and man.

Not much is available in the Bible about Nicolaitans; however it is known that they were a class among Christians, who introduced into the church a false doctrine of false freedom and licentiousness taking undue advantage of misinterpreting Paul's doctrine of grace. (cf. 2 Peter 2:15-19; 1 Corinthians 8:1-13)

Before resorting to any legalism in eating or rejecting the sacrifices offered to idols 1 Corinthians 8:1-13 should be understood clearly.

"That ye abstain from meats offered to idols, and from blood, and from things strangled, and from fornication: from which if ye keep yourselves, ye shall do well. Fare ye well" (Acts 15:29)

"But if any man say unto you, This is offered in sacrifice unto idols, eat not for his sake that shewed it, and for conscience sake: for the earth is the Lord's, and the fulness thereof" (1 Corinthians 10:28)

The Lord hated Nicolaitans who practiced to have mediatorship of their choice rather than having Lord Jesus Christ as mediator.

Bible clearly refuses to have any other mediatorship, such as "shepherding" by pastors, or mediating between sinner and God. The sinner can approach God directly through the mediatorship of Lord Jesus Christ and no other mediator is needed.

"And for this cause he is the mediator of the new testament, that by means of death, for the redemption of the transgressions that were under the first testament, they which are called might receive the promise of eternal inheritance" (Hebrews 9:15)

The Lord sent His message to the church at Pergamum to repent and remove such teachers from among them in order that He may give to them hidden manna and "white stone" as a token of acceptance by Him.

Repent; or else I will come unto thee quickly, and will fight against them with the sword of my mouth. (Revelation 2:16)

"I am that bread of life. Your fathers did eat manna in the wilderness, and are dead. This is the bread which cometh down from heaven, that a man may eat thereof, and not die" (John 6:48-50)

CHAPTER 6
TO THE CHURCH IN THYATIRA

(From Revelation Chapter 2)

Letter to the Church in Thyatira is the fourth letter written by John to the elder of this church at the command of Lord Jesus Christ, "the Son of God, who hath his eyes like unto a flame of fire, and his feet are like fine brass" (cf. Rev. 2:18).

The metal brass in scriptures represents judgment. The Lord will surely judge everyone without any exception. He judges those in the present church that they may repent and return; He judges the children of God in eternity to reward them; and He judges the unsaved to be cast into 'lake of fire'.

Lord Jesus Christ humbled Himself and came into this world in the form of a servant in the likeness of man seeking that which was lost (cf. Luke19:10). John saw Him and said "…"Behold, the Lamb of God, who takes away the sin of the world!" (John 1:29 b ESV)

When He comes again He will no more be like a 'lamb' but will be as the "Lion of the tribe of Judah". He will rule the nations with a "rod of iron". John saw heaven opened and He beheld a white horse and He who was seated on it was called "Faithful and True and in righteousness" He judges and makes war. (cf. Revelation 19:11-12)

While the Lord had great appreciation for the church in Thyatira for their love, faith, service and patient endurance, He was very shrewd in His words and condemned their idolatry and sexual immorality. He does not tolerate idolatry, much less if structures of idols are placed in the church and worship is rendered to them. God is Spirit and He said:

"Ye shall make you no idols nor graven image, neither rear you up a standing image, neither shall ye set up any image of stone in your land, to bow down unto it: for I am the LORD your God" (Leviticus 26:1)

The glory of the LORD departed from Solomon's temple because he loved "many strange women, together with the daughter of Pharaoh, women of the Moabites, Ammonites, Edomites, Zidonians, and Hittites" (Ref. 1 Kings 11:1)

Prophet Ezekiel saw the "glory of the God of Israel" returning to the temple from "the way of the east: His voice was like a voice of many waters: and the earth shined with glory" as prophesied. (Ref. Ezekiel 11:22-23 and Ezekiel 43:2)

The Lord says the latter works of this church in Thyatira will exceed the first. However, He was against this church for its tolerance of the kind of sins that the woman named Jezebel committed. Jezebel was the wife of Ahab, who thought it is of no great significance to marry her, who went and served "Baal" and worshipped him. There is was none like Ahab, who sold himself to wickedness in the sight of the LORD.

She called herself as prophetess and taught seducing of the LORD's servants to worship idols and practice sexual immorality and to eat food sacrificed to idols; thus kindling the anger of the LORD. The church at Thyatira, which practiced these evil deeds, did not repent of that evil. (Ref. 1 Kings 16:31, 1 Kings21:25; Rev. 2:20)

The young man sent by Prophet Elisha anointed Jehu as King over Israel and ordered him to kill Jezebel and prophesied that dogs will eat her (Ref. 2 Kings 9:4-10)

"And the dogs shall eat Jezebel in the portion of Jezreel, and there shall be none to bury her. And he opened the door, and fled" (2 Kings 9:10)

This prophecy was fulfilled when she was thrown down from the window by eunuchs at the orders of Jehu.

"And he said, Throw her down. So they threw her down: and some of her blood was sprinkled on the wall, and on the horses: and he trod her under foot. And when he had come in, he did eat and drink, and said, Go, see now this cursed woman, and bury her: for she is a king's daughter" (2 Kings 9:33-34)

The Lord was very angry with the church in Thyatira and said unless they repented of their deeds, He will cast her into a bed, and them that commit adultery with her into "great tribulation". This church would be on the earth to face "great tribulation" unless they repented of their wickedness. This church is the one that has idols of Mary, and other men, who were called as "Saints" and worship is rendered to them. The Lord says unless they repent of their wickedness, He will kill her children with death and all the churches will know that God searches the minds and hearts of everyone. He gives everyone according to one's works.

Apostle Paul has a message for all of us such as the one that the Lord had through John to the church in Thyatira. Do we presume that we can get along with refusal to repent of our sin depicting contempt towards God's riches in kindness, forbearance and patience? God's kindness is meant to lead us to repentance and not surely to continue in sin. If our hearts are hardened and we remain impenitent we are storing up wrath for ourselves. The Lord shows His righteousness when He returns. He renders each one according to one's own works (Ref. Romans 2:4-6)

The Lord instructs the rest of the members of the church in Thyatira, who do not follow Jezebel's deeds, to hold fast unto their faithfulness toward the Lord until He comes. He promises them the power to rule over the nations; even as that He received of His Father. He commands them to overcome the activities of the devil; the prominent of them are idolatry and sexual immorality.

The Lord promises to give to those who follow Him the "morning star", which is His name (cf. Rev. 22:16), sharing His glory with us, in order that we may shine like Him in perfect brightness. These blessings are as much applicable to us even this day as it was during the days when the letter was written to the church in Thyatira. It is not an ordinary reward to have power over nations even as Lord Jesus received from His Father. He who can understand let Him understand.

"He that has an ear, let him hear what the Spirit says unto the churches" (Revelation 2:29)

CHAPTER 7
TO THE CHURCH IN SARDIS

(From Revelation Chapter 3)

"And unto the angel of the church in Sardis write; These things saith he that hath the seven Spirits of God, and the seven stars; I know thy works, that thou hast a name that thou livest, and art dead" (Revelation 3:1).

In the first chapter of Revelation Lord Jesus Christ revealed that the seven stars in His hand are seven angels (i.e. seven ministers, or pastors, or elders or leaders) in the church, and seven candlesticks (lamps) are seven churches; and the seven spirits (seven being the full number in Scriptures) signifies Holy Spirit.

The Lord identified Himself in letter to the church in Ephesus as "who holds the seven stars in his right hand, who walks among the seven golden lampstands"; as "the first and the last, who died and came to life" to the church in Smyrna; as the one "who has the sharp two-edged sword" to the church as Pergamum; as "the Son of God, who hath his eyes like unto a flame of fire, and his feet are like fine brass" to the church at Thyatira; and as "he that hath the seven Spirits of God, and the seven stars" in the letter to the church in Sardis.

Sardis is of much importance because it is from here that Xerxes invaded Greece and Cyrus marched against his brother Artaxerxes. Cyrus and Artaxerxes played important role in building Zerubbabel temple and Jerusalem city. It is also of interest because it is the home of one of the Seven Churches of Rev (1:11; 3:1).

The Lord warned the church in Sardis, who were spiritually dead, to wake up and strengthen themselves spiritually instead of allowing the remains of faith to die. Jesus Christ, who is the head of the Church, looks after the church and that which goes on in the church. He conveys His messages and directions to the elders and the members of the church and controls them.

Here is an admonition to them that the Lord, who is the head of the church, did not find their works complete in the sight of His Father, whom He calls here as "my God". He instructs the elders to keep the word of God that they received and to repent of their failures.

At the turn-point of time when Protestant movement was at its ripe, there came a period when the church was dead inwardly. It was like sepulcher that looked pretty white outwardly; but smelled bad internally. They were very active in respect of building monumental structures known for external beauty but were devoid of spiritual knowledge. It was similar to what the Lord said about the church in Sardis. The Lord said He knew their works that they are dead while they live.

Paul addressed the issue of being dead while living and writes to Timothy in his first epistle 5th Chapter that the widow who is self-indulgent is dead even while she lives. (cf. 1Timothy 5:6)

James comes down heavily on rich ones that their miseries shall come upon them because they nourished their hearts with pleasure and for gathering riches for their last days. It is because they did not live for the Lord that their gold and silver was cankered, and the rust on them was witness against them. (cf. James 5:1-5)

There is a lesson here for the present generation to take. Complying with the instructions of the Lord as it is written in Matthew 10:23, Paul and Timothy preached Gospel in one city and fled to another when persecution came along.

"When they persecute you in one town, flee to the next, for truly, I say to you, you will not have gone through all the towns of Israel before the Son of Man comes" (Matthew 10:23 ESV)

Later Paul writes to Timothy that he endured persecutions and sufferings for the sake of Gospel and in order that the latter may follow his way of preaching advises him to continue in the teachings that he learnt.

"But thou hast fully known my doctrine, manner of life, purpose, faith, longsuffering, charity, patience, Persecutions, afflictions, which came unto me at Antioch, at Iconium, at Lystra; what persecutions I endured: but out of them all the Lord delivered me. Yea, and all that will live godly in Christ Jesus shall suffer persecution. But evil men and seducers shall wax worse and worse, deceiving, and being deceived. But continue thou in the things which thou hast learned and hast been assured of, knowing of whom thou hast learned them" (2 Timothy 3:10-14)

The Lord warns churches that if they do not wake up and stand up to His expectations, He will come like a thief at an hour unknown to anyone. He warned His disciples earlier that the owner of a house could avoid burglary by thief by keeping close watch. The Lord's coming for the Church, which is His bride, will be at quite unexpected time, and therefore, He warns every Christian to be watchful entire time; lest they should lose their possessions.

"But know this, that if the master of the house had known in what part of the night the thief was coming, he would have stayed awake and would not have let his house be broken into" (Matthew 24:43 ESV)

However, He acknowledges that there are some who did not go back from holding fast to the scriptures they listened to and read. The Lord says about them as those who have "not soiled their garments". They walk with the Lord in white garments (indicative of holiness) that they are worthy of His company. He promises them that He will clothe the one who conquers in white garments and will not blot out his name from the book of life. (cf. Revelation 7:9). The Lord confesses before the Father and His angels all those who confess His name before men.

"Whosoever therefore shall confess me before men, him will I confess also before my Father which is in heaven" (Matthew 10:32)

Finally the Lord Jesus Christ says "He who has an ear, let him hear what the Spirit says to the churches" (addressing all churches here).

CHAPTER 8
TO THE CHURCH IN PHILADELPHIA

(From Revelation Chapter 3)

Philadelphia was an ancient city located in Lydia about 20 miles south of Sardis, and about 100 miles south of Smyrna. The message to this church covers the church history period from around 1750 AD to 1900 AD. This church is historically significant because it is in this period that the doctrine of the Pre-tribulation Rapture ("caught up") of the church, and the period of "Great tribulation" are identified and taught by theologians by about 1850 AD.

The church and the church age was mystery in the Old Testament period. There are many such mysteries revealed as the years passed by. Daniel was asked to shut up the prophecy until the last days.

"But thou, O Daniel, shut up the words, and seal the book, even to the time of the end: many shall run to and fro, and knowledge shall be increased" (Daniel 12:4)

Lord Jesus Christ sends His message through John, who wrote this letter to the church in Philadelphia, which is sixth in sequence. This is the only church in which Lord Jesus was pleased and expressed His full happiness. The Lord has the seven Spirits of God and the seven ministers of God. (Seven in scriptures being the number of fullness the seven spirits here refer to the Holy Spirit).

Earlier John wrote that the Son of God came into this world and gave us an understanding that we may know Him, who is true, and that we are in Him. Jesus Christ, the Son of God, is the way, the truth and the life (Cf. 1 John 5:20; John 14:6)

The promise made by Lord Jesus with the church is similar to the promise that Jehovah made with Jacob. As Jacob was precious in the sight of the LORD, and had been honorable, He loved him, and therefore, He said He would give men for him and people for his life (cf. Isaiah 43:4)

The church is the body of Christ upon this earth and after rapture the church will be His bride. Lord Jesus Christ, who is from the lineage of David, has the key to open the door, which no man can shut when He opens; and no one can open when He shuts. He also holds the key to death and Hades. The promise of the Father is that the Son will be given the key, (which signifies the authority), to the house of David and His kingdom shall be everlasting.

"And the key of the house of David will I lay upon his shoulder; so he shall open, and none shall shut; and he shall shut, and none shall open" (Isaiah 22:22)

The Angel said to Virgin Mary that she was found favor with God…"And behold, you will conceive in your womb and bear a son, and you shall call his name Jesus. He will be great and will be called the Son of the Most High. And the Lord God will give to him the throne of his father David, and he will reign over the house of Jacob forever, and of his kingdom there will be no end." (Luke 1:31-33 ESV)

The Lord says that He sets an open door before the church in Philadelphia that they may, even with their little strength, may have opportunity to do greater service to Him. He appreciates them that even though they had little strength they kept the word of God and have not denied His name.

Apostle Paul may have thought that if he had greater strength than he had he would do better service to the Lord and therefore, prayed to remove the thorn in his flesh; but the Lord said to him that in his weakness was the Lord's strength manifest (2 Corinthians 12:7-10).

If we consider that the door mentioned here is for salvation, then we miss the gist of message. The church has already saved ones and the demand here is for their greater service to the Lord. (cf. Acts 14:27; 1 Corinthians 16:9; 2 Corinthians 2:12; and Colossians 4:3)

The Lord says those Jews, who denied Him in the Synagogue calling themselves as Jews, are the synagogue of Satan. There will come a time when Jews who denied Jesus as their Messiah, will to come to the feet of the church and, will know that He loved the church.

"The sons also of them that afflicted thee shall come bending unto thee; and all they that despised thee shall bow themselves down at the soles of thy feet; and they shall call thee, The city of the LORD, The Zion of the Holy One of Israel" (Isaiah 60:14)

Another great promise the Lord made with the church in Philadelphia is that it is because they kept the word of His patience, He will keep them from the hour of temptation. The reference is here to the "great tribulation", which will come upon the entire world to try them that live upon the earth. The Lord will keep the church out from this "great tribulation".

Speaking to Peter Jesus said the gates of hell shall not prevail against the church that He builds upon Himself. (cf. Matthew 16:18)

"And I say also unto thee, That thou art Peter, and upon this rock I will build my church; and the gates of hell shall not prevail against it" (Matthew 16:18)

The Lord promises that He will come quickly and, therefore, commands them to hold fast to the word of God and the truth in order that no man may snatch away their crown. He who overcomes will be made a pillar in the temple of the Lord and he shall not go out of His presence anymore. The Lord will write His new name upon Him.

"The one who conquers, I will make him a pillar in the temple of my God. Never shall he go out of it, and I will write on him the name of my God, and the name of the city of my God, the new Jerusalem, which comes down from my God out of heaven, and my own new name" (Revelation 3:12 ESV)

"then the Lord knows how to rescue the godly from trials, and to keep the unrighteous under punishment until the day of judgment" (2 Peter 2:9 ESV)

"He, who has an ear, let him hear what the Spirit says to the churches." (Revelation 3:6 ESV)

CHAPTER 9
TO THE CHURCH IN LAODICEA

(From Revelation Chapter 2)

"And to the angel of the church in Laodicea write: 'The words of the Amen, the faithful and true witness, the beginning of God's creation. 'I know your works: you are neither cold nor hot. Would that you were either cold or hot! So, because you are lukewarm, and neither hot nor cold, I will spit you out of my mouth' " (Revelation 3:14-16 ESV)

Laodicea was the wealthiest city located in the valley of Lycos of Asia Minor in the country Phrygia. In Paul's letter to Colossians and 1Timothy he refers to Laodicea (cf. Colossians 2:1; 4:13, 15-16; 1Timothy 6:21). It gives us much scope to assume they were very close in their culture. The church in Laodicea started in about 60 AD when Paul was preaching Gospel to the church at Ephesus. Later, false teaching crept into their church as into the church at Colossae.

Paul warned of Oriental or Gnostic philosophy that prevailed in Laodicea and Colossae during those days. He warned them to be careful that no man may deceive them by tradition of men and after the rudiments of the world. Their Philosophy promoted speculation, respecting nature of divine presence. Colossians relied much on reasoning than that was taught by Christian teachers.

"And when this epistle is read among you, cause that it be read also in the church of the Laodiceans; and that ye likewise read the epistle from Laodicea" (Colossians 4:16)

"Beware lest any man spoil you through philosophy and vain deceit, after the tradition of men, after the rudiments of the world, and not after Christ" (Colossians 2:8)

Laodicea suffered massive earthquake in AD 60 and the church was recovering from it. While other cities around this city in Phrygia also suffered massive earthquake they rebuilt their cities with the financial support from Roman Government. However, the city Laodicea did not seek financial support from Roman Government but it rebuilt its city with their finances. It had a very fertile ground for the sheep which were bred to produce soft glossy black wool. Laodicea had very prosperous textile industry, a very renowned school of medicine, and yet it had great shortage water supply.

Jesus identified as "Amen" while addressing the church in Laodicea. The word "Amen" means "surely" or "trustworthy" or "so be it". Jesus is the "faithful and true witness, the beginning of God's creation". He was not a created being but He was the creator.

The message from Jesus conveyed by a letter to the church in Laodicea was seventh in sequence. Although the letter was written in about 96 AD, It had a prophetical message for the present generation and the churches now in existence.

Even though Laodicea was very rich in every respect they lacked life sustaining water. Laodicea had to depend on a city on the north of it called "Hierapolis" that had warm water, and on "Colossae" on the south side that had cold water. They drew water from those cities for their need. However, by the time warm water came from the north to their city it lost its warmth. Likewise by the time the cold water came to their city from south it lost is cold nature. The water from the north was not helpful to them because it was lukewarm when it was available to them in their city. Likewise the water from the south was not helpful to them because it became lukewarm and lost its refreshing nature by the time it came to their city from south.

The reference to "lukewarm" in this passage was not about attitude of worship they had. It does not say that they neither had high attitude of spirited worship nor had very low attitude to worship. All that it refers to is that they did not serve the primary purposes that they were chosen for. Jesus says He will spew them out from His mouth because they were neither hot nor cold but were lukewarm.

The church in Laodicea took pride in their wealth but did not realize how poor, blind they were spiritually. They were in wretched and pitiable condition. Jesus counsels them to buy from Him gold (indicative of spirit-filled life from Him) that was refined by fire that they may truly become rich in heaven; white garments, which represent holiness in order that they may clothe and cover their shame so as not to be as naked (figurative of their poverty) before others in heaven; for none is naked or unholy in heaven. They took pride in medicine that was available to them, but Jesus says to them to buy eye-salve to anoint their eyes that they may see clearly. He reproves and disciplines them that He loves; and therefore, He advises them to be zealous and repent.

Jesus is outside of this church and knocking on their door that they may open it for Him that He may enter and if anyone opens the door He will come in and eat with him. He grants to the one who conquers the worldly life and false teaching, the privilege to sit with Him on His throne, as He conquered and sat down with His Father on His throne.

"Behold, I stand at the door and knock. If anyone hears my voice and opens the door, I will come in to him and eat with him, and he with me. The one who conquers, I will grant him to sit with me on my throne, as I also conquered and sat down with my Father on his throne" (Revelation 3:20-21 ESV)

Finally the Lord says:

"He, who has an ear, let him hear what the Spirit says to the churches."

CHAPTER 10
THE THRONE IN HEAVEN

From Revelation Chapter 4

"After this I looked, and behold, a door standing open in heaven! And the first voice, which I had heard speaking to me like a trumpet, said, 'Come up here, and I will show you what must take place after this.' " (Revelation 4:1 ESV)

John wrote seven letters to the seven churches, in Asia Minor, and the fulfillment thereof was seen historically over a period from about AD 96 to AD 1900 and onward. He writes in Chapter 4 about the"Throne of God" in heaven. Two times the words "meta tauta" translated from Greek i.e. "After this" or "hereafter" occur in the very first verse indicating that he was writing this chapter surely after he wrote to the seven letters to the seven churches at the command of God. This also reminds us of the Lord Jesus Christ's words which read...

"Write the things which thou hast seen, and the things which are, and the things which shall be hereafter" (Revelation 1:19)

John was taken in the Spirit on the Lord's Day, when he was commanded to write the things that he saw in his vision, and the things that were, when he wrote seven letters to the seven churches, and the things that shall come to pass thereafter. The things that he saw were recorded in Revelation chapter 1. In Revelation chapters 2 and 3 were recorded the things that were, and in Revelation chapters 4 to 22 are recorded of the things that shall come to pass thereafter.

John saw a door standing open in heaven and the first voice that he heard was like a trumpet saying to him "Come up here, and I will show you what must take place after this." He was in the Spirit immediately, and saw one seated on the throne in heaven. Trumpets were used in Old Testament period to call attention of multitudes of people, or an individual for specific purpose. Moses heard the trumpet sound when God called him on to the top of Mount Sinai where he received from God the "Ten Commandments".

The children of Israel were called by the sounding the trumpet in different tunes for different purposes; the call could be to gather to wage war or face war etc. More incidences of trumpet usage can be found in these references... Ex 19:13,16,19; 20:18; Le 25:9; Nu 10:4; Jos 6:5,20; Judg. 3:27; 6:34; 7:16,18; 20:37; 1Sa 13:3; 2Sa 2:28; 6:15; 15:10; 18:16; 20:1,22; 1Ki 1:34,39,41; Ne 4:18,20; Job 39:24; Ps 47:5; 81:3; 150:3; Isa 18:3; 27:13; 58:1; Jer. 4:5,19,21; 6:1,17; 42:14; 51:27; Ezek. 7:14; 33:3-6; Ho 5:8; 8:1; Joe 2:1,15; Am 2:2; 3:6; Zeph. 1:16; Zech. 9:14.

There are two important verses in the New Testament where the usage of Trumpet is found. One is in 1 Corinthians 15:52 which reads...

"In a moment, in the twinkling of an eye, at the last trump: for the trumpet shall sound, and the dead shall be raised incorruptible, and we shall be changed" (1 Corinthians 15:52)

Another important occasion is when the"...Lord himself shall descend from heaven with a shout, with the voice of the archangel, and with the trump of God: and the dead in Christ shall rise first: Then we which are alive and remain shall be caught up together with them in the clouds, to meet the Lord in the air: and so shall we ever be with the Lord" (1 Thessalonians 4:16-17)

Irrespective of where the event of 'catching up' of the church is placed in the timeline of Daniel's 70-Week-prophesy for understanding purposes, the 'catching away' of the Church is undisputed. The word "Rapture" is not found in the Bible; however the word is commonly used to refer to the word used as "Caught up" in 1 Thessalonians 4:16-17. Except for the view "pre-tribulation rapture" any other view seems untenable in the light of the fact that Revelation was written in about AD 96, and the mystery of the Church was unknown in the Old Testament period.

The first verse of Revelation chapter 4 gives ample evidence that the church is "caught up" when John saw of the things that were to come to pass in future. He made a reference to the twenty-four elders, who are human beings, wearing crowns that they earned for themselves, were seated on their thrones.

Apostle Paul explains in Hebrews chapters 8, 9 and 13 that there was a tabernacle made in the Old Testament period, by Moses at the command of the LORD and that tabernacle was shadow of the things to come.

"Who serve unto the example and shadow of heavenly things, as Moses was admonished of God when he was about to make the tabernacle: for, See, saith he, that thou make all things according to the pattern shewed to thee in the mount" (Hebrews 8:5)

The throne room where the LORD is seated on His throne is like the model of the Tabernacle that we know from its description. In the "Most Holy" place of the tabernacle was the "ark of the covenant of the Lord". The LORD's throne in heaven is similar to the mercy seat upon the "ark of the covenant of the LORD" in the "Most Holy Place". It was on the Mercy seat that the glory of the LORD appeared and spoke to Moses and Aaron.

The one who was seated on the throne in heaven "had the appearance of jasper and carnelian and around the throne was a rainbow that had the appearance of an emerald". That description presents the Majesty and beautiful-look of the LORD in heaven.

There were twenty four smaller thrones around the LORD's throne, and on these thrones were seated twenty four elders. These twenty-four elders clothed in white garments, significant of purity and the holiness, represent the church which is 'caught up' to be with the Lord for ever and ever. There is a promise given to the church in Laodicea in Revelation chapter 3:21 that says:

"The one who conquers, I will grant him to sit with me on my throne, as I also conquered and sat down with my Father on his throne" (Revelation 3:21 ESV)

The twenty-four elders are human beings and are "kings and priests", who have on their heads crowns of gold (Greek Strong's# 4735 Stephanos, which are earned in sports; not "diadems" which are ornamental worn by the kings, who are royal by nature). The golden crowns worn by them are emblematic and symbolic of the saved people of God. (cf. Revelation 5:10)

"And hast made us unto our God kings and priests: and we shall reign on the earth" (Revelation 5:10)

The seven candlesticks in the "Holy place" in the Tabernacle represent seven spirits of God, the Holy Spirit. In heaven flashes of lightning and rumblings of peals of thunder came from the throne before which were seven spirits of God, and these seven spirits of God were the seven works of the Holy Spirit. There was as it were a sea of glass like crystal before the throne.

There were four living creatures one on each side of the throne and they were full of eyes, in front and behind, indicative of full of wisdom.

The first living creature was like a lion, indicative of the "Lion of the tribe of Judah", who is none other than Lord Jesus Christ Himself, and of whom Matthew's Gospel speaks.

The second living creature was like an ox, indicative of "suffering servant" as prophesied in Isaiah Chapter 53, and of whom Mark's Gospel speaks.

The third living creature was "with the face of a man", indicative of Lord Jesus Christ, the "Son of man", who relinquished His glory with the Father and came to this world in the likeness of man.

The fourth living creature was like an eagle in flight, indicative of all powerful Lord Jesus Christ, the "Son of God", of whom the Gospel of John speaks.

Each of the four living creatures had six wings and they were full of eyes all around and within and all of them collectively praised God never ceasing to say...

"Holy, holy, holy, is the Lord God Almighty, who was and is and is to come!"

The LORD's majesty is also seen in Ezekiel chapters1 and 10 and Isaiah Chapter 6

And when the four living creatures gave glory, honor and thanks to the LORD who lives forever and ever, the twenty four elders fell down before Him and worshipped Him. As they worship the LORD, who lives forever and ever, they cast their crowns, in honor of the LORD, and say...

"Thou art worthy, O Lord, to receive glory and honour and power: for thou hast created all things, and for thy pleasure they are and were created" (Revelation 4:11)

The LORD is worthy to receive glory, honor, and power, because He created all things, and for His pleasure they were and are created. There is, therefore, no doubt that we human beings are created for His pleasure and to worship Him. Satan set his heart as the heart of God and in his pride considered himself as God and the result was that he fell from the presence of the LORD. There is no salvation for Satan. He and his angels will be cast into 'lake of fire' after the 'great white throne' judgment.

Choose either to worship God or Satan to receive salvation and be with the Lord for ever and ever or alternatively receive damnation to be cast into the 'lake of fire'. There is no midway to escape from worshipping. When we cease to worship the LORD we cease to serve His purposes and pleasures. It is imperative, therefore, that we realize this fact. Salvation is never lost; receive this gift today and worship the LORD who lives forever and ever.

CHAPTER 11
THE SCROLL OPENED

From Revelation Chapter 5

The events leading to the unveiling of the future and redemption of the earth are recorded in this chapter. The title-deed to the earth is to be opened by the only worthy one, who is Lord Jesus Christ, "the Lion of the tribe of Judah", the root of David. Jesus came into the world as the "Lamb of God" and died on behalf of us. God raised Him from the dead and He was on this earth for forty days before His ascension, and then He ascended into heaven.

John in his vision saw a scroll in the right of the LORD, who sat on His throne. He lives forever and ever. The scroll had writing within and without and it was the title-deed to the earth.

God created heavens and earth and gave it over to man to replenish and subdue it. He gave man a wife and blessed man and woman to be fruitful and multiply and said to them to have dominion over the fish of the sea, and over the birds of the heavens and over every living that moves on the earth (cf. Genesis 1:28)

Satan was crafty and tempted Eve to eat of the forbidden fruit of the tree of knowledge of the good and the evil in the Garden of Eden. She not only ate it but gave it to her husband, who also ate of it. Thus by transgressing the commandment of God they lost earth to Satan and earned death for themselves.

It had cost God very dearly. He sent His only Son, Jesus into this world, in order to reconcile man and earth for Himself. It pleased the Father to bruise His only Son to redeem not only man but also the earth to Himself. Jesus died on the cross a substitutionary death to redeem mankind from sin.

"For God so loved the world, that he gave his only begotten Son, that whosoever believeth in him should not perish, but have everlasting life" (John 3:16)

Apostle Paul quoted Psalm 24:1 and said that the earth is the Lord's and the fullness thereof (cf. 1 Corinthians 10:26). Indeed, the earth is the Lord's and all that is therein. The Lord causes storms, thunders, rains, sunshine, plants to grow, animals to procreate and so on... However, the activities of the world such as sin that dominates men, who have not yielded to God, lack of love toward God and neighbor, hatred, anger, sexual immorality, greed for wealth, fleshly pleasure, seeking power to control others, or other nations etc., are all under the control of Satan. He who overcomes will be blessed by God.

When Jesus was about to commence His ministry on this earth, the devil approached Him and tempted Him to worship him and if He did so, the devil said, he would give the entire world and all that is in the world to Him. Lord Jesus Christ did not dispute that the earth was His and the fullness thereof; rather He thwarted away the devil by citing scriptures from the Old Testament. This is evidence that the earth is presently under the control of Satan and it is yet to be redeemed.

Paul says Satan has blinded the minds of men that they may not understand the glorious gospel of Jesus Christ; lest they should believe in Him, who is the image of God (cf. 2 Corinthians 4:4)

John in his vision saw an angel proclaiming with a loud voice as to who is worthy to open the book and unloosen the seven seals of the book. The book contained the acts that were going to be performed in order to redeem the earth and punish the devil. Satan will be crushed fully by God in order for Him to redeem the earth from its bondage.

Old Testament Law provides solutions for redeeming the land on the seventh year, the slave on the seventh year etc. (cf. Exod. 21:1-31). The same application would, perhaps, be made in redeeming the earth. It is already six thousand years passed after the earth has gone to be under the control of Satan We do not know the date and time of the coming of Jesus Christ but the redemption is imminent. We are asked to look forward for His coming eagerly. Those who are left-behind will have only seven year period, or less before the Lord steps physically on the Mount of Olives and makes His second advent on the earth.

When the angel cried out loudly as to who was there to open the scroll there was no man in heaven or on the earth, who was worthy to open or to look at the book. John wept because there was no man found worthy to open the book. Then, one of the twenty four elders, who were representatives of the church, redeemed and made righteous by the blood of Lord Jesus Christ, said to him not to weep because "the Lion of the tribe of Judah", the root of David has prevailed the enemy and overcome the world and He is worthy to open the seven seals of the book. Lord Jesus Christ was the only one who was worthy to open the book and He is the Son of God.

John saw in his vision the Lamb standing as though it had been slain and now alive, in the midst of the throne and the four living creatures, and in the midst of the elders. (John pointed in his Gospel that Jesus was the "Lamb of God" who takes away the sin of the world [cf. John 1:29; John 1:36]). He saw the

Lamb having seven horns which represent fullness in the authority, and seven eyes that represent fullness in wisdom. These seven horns and seven eyes are the seven Spirits of God that represent the Holy Spirit, who was sent forth into the entire earth. Holy Spirit dwells in believers' hearts continually. He is our comforter and convicts us of our sin and provides a way out from temptations.

Lord Jesus Christ took the book out of the right hand of the Father who sat on the throne. As soon as the Lord took the book from the hand of the LORD on the throne, the four living creatures and twenty four elders fell down before Him. They had one harp each and golden bowls full of incense, which are the prayers of the saints. They all sang a new song, saying,

"Worthy are you to take the scroll and to open its seals, for you were slain, and by your blood you ransomed people for God from every tribe and language and people and nation, and you have made them a kingdom and priests to our God, and they shall reign on the earth." (Revelation 5:9-10 ESV)

John looked and heard, "around the throne and the living creatures and the elders the voice of many angels, numbering myriads of myriads and thousands of thousands, saying with a loud voice, "Worthy is the Lamb who was slain, to receive power and wealth and wisdom and might and honor and glory and blessing!" (Revelation 5:11-12 ESV)

The prophecy of Daniel is fulfilled here. He wrote: "A stream of fire issued and came out from before him; a thousand thousands served him, and ten thousand times ten thousand stood before him; the court sat in judgment, and the books were opened" Daniel 7:10

John heard every creature in heaven and on earth and under the earth and in the sea and all that is in them saying, "To him who sits on the throne and to the Lamb be blessing and honor and glory and might forever and ever!"

"And the four living creatures said, "Amen!" and the elders fell down and worshiped" (Revelation 5:13-14 ESV)

THE SEVEN SEALS

CHAPTER 12
THE FIRST SEAL

From Revelation Chapter 6

"Now I watched when the Lamb opened one of the seven seals, and I heard one of the four living creatures say with a voice like thunder, "Come!" And I looked, and behold, a white horse! And its rider had a bow, and a crown was given to him, and he came out conquering, and to conquer" (Revelation 6:1-2 ESV)

Lord Jesus Christ was only one found worthy to take the scroll from the LORD, who lives forever and ever, and open it. That the scroll was written inside and out and sealed with seven seals is indicative of importance legally.

With the opening of the first seal, the seventh week of Daniel's seventy-week prophecy begins to unfold. This is the final week in the prophecy and at the end of seventieth week Lord Jesus Christ will step on the Mount of Olives along with the church that was 'caught up' to Him and along with many angels. The first four seals of the seven seals correspond to the events of the first phase of 3.5 years of 70th week and the last three seals of the seven seals correspond to the 'Great Tribulation' which lasts for 3.5 years. The last phase of 3.5 could be cut short at the discretion of Lord Jesus Christ in order reduce the persecution of Jews (Cf. Matt. 24:22). Daniel was told that the words are closed up and sealed till the time of the end.

"And except those days should be shortened, there should no flesh be saved: but for the elect's sake those days shall be shortened" (Matthew 24:22)

And he said, Go thy way, Daniel: for the words are closed up and sealed till the time of the end. (Daniel 12:9)

As we understand from prophecy in Daniel 12:11-13 there are thirty more days after the final 7-year-period, when 'sheep and goat' judgment would take place, and forty five days thereafter the literal millennial kingdom would be set up by Lord Jesus Christ, who would rule all the nations from the throne of David in Jerusalem.

We see a pattern of unfolding of the events. Out of seven seals of the scroll six seals are opened consecutively and before the seventh seal is opened there is an interlude. Next, seven trumpets are blown; however, after six trumpets are blown there is an interlude. Next, seven vials are poured upon the earth; however between the time of blowing of sixth trumpet and the seventh trumpet there are "seven thunders" are seen in Revelation Chapter 10. The interlude between the sixth trumpet and the seventh is not one chapter but a group of chapters from Revelation 10 to 14.

The description of opening of the six seals out of seven seals is described in Revelation chapter 6 and after an interlude of one chapter, i.e. 7th Chapter, where it is recorded about the sealing of 144,000, the seventh seal is opens as recorded in Revelation chapter 8.

Apostle Paul writes about Apostasy and Antichrist in 2 Thessalonians 2:2-10. After apostasy is set in the restrainer, who is the Holy Spirit, is moved out of the way. It is at this time that the 'man of sin', who is also called 'son of perdition' is revealed. He is the Antichrist.

As John watched he saw the Lamb opening one of the seven seals. Whenever a seal is opened one of the four living creatures heralds an important event. As Lord Jesus opens the first seal one of the four living creatures announces of the white horse that is on the run with its rider, who has a bow, and a crown that was given to him. The rider on the white horse goes on conquering and to conquer.

There are varied opinions as to who this rider on the white horse is. Going by the general interpretation that the color "white" represents righteousness of Christ, one would think that the rider is Jesus, but as the details are perused, it is evident that the rider is not Jesus; but he was an imposter. At this stage, when the rider on the white horse was on the run, Lord Jesus was opening the seal and not riding the horse. The imposter, who was riding the horse, was Antichrist who went on conquering and to conquer with his falsehood. He goes on blaspheming God and sets himself in the temple of God and proclaims that he is the God.

"Let no one deceive you in any way. For that day will not come, unless the rebellion comes first, and the man of lawlessness is revealed, the son of destruction, who opposes and exalts himself against every so-called god or object of worship, so that he takes his seat in the temple of God, proclaiming himself to be God" (2 Thessalonians 2:3-4 ESV)

Beware of sprit of antichrist now prevailing, Antichrist who is yet to come, False Prophets and False witnesses already there now in the world.

"For there are certain men crept in unawares, who were before of old ordained to this condemnation, ungodly men, turning the grace of our God into lasciviousness, and denying the only Lord God, and our Lord Jesus Christ" (Jude 1:4)

CHAPTER 13
SECOND SEAL OPENED

(From Revelation Chapter 6)

It is interesting to note that whenever an event in heaven has to happen it is announced by one of the twenty-four elders; but whenever an event that has to happen on earth it is announced by one of the four living creatures.

It was one of the elders who announced that Lord Jesus Christ was the only one found worthy to open the seals of the scroll, which was a legal document to regain the earth back to the Father. There was no man found worthy to open it. When the first seal was opened one of the living creatures announced of the entrance of an imposter, who is Antichrist on his white horse onto the earth to commence his reign of the last week of Daniel's seventy-week prophecy.

As the second seal on the scroll is opened by Lord Jesus Christ, the second living creature announces of the entrance of one who is empowered to take away peace from the earth. The second horse that comes onto the earth is bright red in color, which signifies that there will be blood-shed on the earth, and its rider is given a sword as an emblem of authority. It is so easy for the second rider to cause wars because all that he has to do is nothing but take away peace from the earth; and there follows wars and turmoil as a consequence.

Nations rise against nations and there will be heavy blood-shed. The opening of the second seal marks the onset of wars and disasters on the earth. The wrath of the LORD begins at the opening of the first seal itself; however the "great tribulation" begins at the second half of the seventieth week of Daniel's prophecy.

The first four seals of the seven seals open before the mid-point of the last week of Daniel's seventy week prophecy (Daniel's prophecy is 7weeks+62 weeks = 69 weeks [when Messiah was cut off]+ 1week). The church era, which was a mystery in the Old Testament period, has come in between 69th week and 70th week with Lord Jesus showing mercy on Gentiles, who along with Jews have become the "One New Man". The details are described in my book "Second Coming of Jesus").

There are differing views about the "day of the Lord", that it is not 24-hour-period; or 3 ½ year period, or 7 year period; however, one consistent view is that God's wrath on earth and earth-dwellers is for seven years, of which the "great Tribulation" is for 3 ½ years during the last half of 70th week of Daniel's 70-week-prophecy.

"For then shall be great tribulation, such as was not since the beginning of the world to this time, no, nor ever shall be" (Matthew 24:21)

According to 1 Thessalonians 5:2 and 2Peter 3:10 "the day of the Lord" comes as a thief in the night and it is not surely for 24-hour period, but it commences with the rapture of the church and would go beyond 'great tribulation', millennial reign of Christ, and until "heavens shall pass away with a great noise, and the elements shall melt with fervent heat, the earth also and the works that are therein shall be burned up".

The phrase the "day of the Lord" is used several times in the Bible indicating the day of vengeance, prominent ones of which are as we read in Ezekiel 13:5; Ezekiel 30:3; Joel 1:15; Joel 2:1; Joel 2:11; Joel 2:31; Joel 3:14; Amos 5:18; Amos 5:20; Obadiah 1:15; Zephaniah 1:7; Zephaniah 1:14; Zephaniah 1:18; Malachi 4:5

"For yourselves know perfectly that the day of the Lord so cometh as a thief in the night" (1 Thessalonians 5:2)

CHAPTER 14
THIRD SEAL OPENED

From Revelation Chapter 6:5-6

"When he opened the third seal, I heard the third living creature say, "Come!" And I looked, and behold, a black horse! And its rider had a pair of scales in his hand. And I heard what seemed to be a voice in the midst of the four living creatures, saying, 'A quart of wheat for a denarius, and three quarts of barley for a denarius, and do not harm the oil and wine!' "(Revelation 6:5-6 ESV)

John in his vision saw four living creatures, as written in Revelation Chapter 4:7; the first one was like a lion, indicative of the Majesty of Jesus, who is the "Lion of the tribe of Judah", as Matthew Gospel recorded about Him, the second one was like an ox, indicative of the suffering servant as prophet Isaiah and Mark's Gospel recorded about Him, the third one was with a face of man indicating that He is the "Son of man"; and He was human in his nature, when He was on this earth", as Luke's Gospel projects Him, and the fourth one was like that of an eagle, indicative of Lord's power and as He is the "Son of God"; and He was divine in nature, when He was on this earth, as the Gospel of John projects Him.

As the third seal was opened the third living creature i.e. one with a face of man, announced of the entrance of a black horse onto the earth. Its rider had a pair of scales in his hand to measure and weigh. (Different colored horses and riders mentioned in Zechariah chapter 1 and 6 do not tie with the horses John saw in his vision and therefore, they are neither same nor identical).

The black horse and its rider mentioned in Revelation chapter 6 are unique and they give us an image that they represent scarcity during calamities. The voice in the midst of the four living creatures said "...A measure of wheat for a penny, and three measures of barley for a penny; and see thou hurt not the oil and the wine" (Revelation 6:6)

"Measure" is translated from Greek word "choenix" which is equivalent to one wine quart and the twelfth part of a quart. Measuring food items and giving them at high prices shows scarcity of items. This happens usually because of wars or God's anger toward men. It is obvious that countries which have acute shortage of food are not blessed; and God's wrath is not far away on countries or individuals who work against His commandments and statues.

A shekel was about 2/5 ounce or 11 grams; A hin was about 4 quarts or 3.5 liters. It would take one day's wages of someone if one wishes to buy food items in little quantity.

It took God to send His prophet Ezekiel to bear the iniquity of the House of Israel to lie upon one of his sides for 390 days; and to bear the iniquity of the House of Judah on the other side for forty days and eat rationed food. Yet, they rejected Lord Jesus, who alone is the savior (Ref. John 14:6).

It took God to send His only Son Lord Jesus Christ, who tasted savor vinegar while on the cross, suffered for our sake, and died a substitutionary death on behalf of us, in order that we may receive salvation free of cost. Now, in future rationing of food items on the earth is sure. Scarcity of it will be felt by every dweller on the earth after the church is 'caught up'. The Jews will realize that Lord Jesus Christ was the true Messiah, who came to save them. (cf. Ezekiel 4:1-11; Ezekiel 5:10, 16; John 19:1-42; Romans 14:11; Phil.2:11; Rev. 1:7; Rev. 13:17-18)

"Take thou also unto thee wheat, and barley, and beans, and lentiles, and millet, and fitches, and put them in one vessel, and make thee bread thereof, according to the number of the days that thou shalt lie upon thy side, three hundred and ninety days shalt thou eat thereof. And thy meat which thou shalt eat shall be by weight, twenty shekels a day: from time to time shalt thou eat it. Thou shalt drink also water by measure, the sixth part of an hin: from time to time shalt thou drink. And thou shalt eat it as barley cakes, and thou shalt bake it with dung that cometh out of man, in their sight" (Ezekiel 4:9-12)

However, the rider on the black horse is commanded not to harm oil and the wine indicating that the nicer things will still be available for people who yield to Him in obedience and worship Him. Oil is used for anointing and for solemn purposes. Prophet Elisha blessed widow to pay her debt with the oil that stayed in her vessels as a result of his blessing. Wine symbolizes wealth and riches. The wine is used in Lord's Supper; and while it is true that large quantity of wine is abuse, it is also true that small quantity of it is useful for medicinal purposes (cf. Genesis 28:18; Exo.25:6;Lev.10:7; 1Samuel 16:13; 1Kings 1:39; 2 Kings 4:1-7; 1 Timothy 5:23)

"And I heard a voice in the midst of the four beasts say, A measure of wheat for a penny, and three measures of barley for a penny; and see thou hurt not the oil and the wine" (Revelation 6:6)

CHAPTER 15
FOURTH SEAL OPENED

(From Revelation 6:7-8)

"And when he had opened the fourth seal, I heard the voice of the fourth beast say, Come and see. And I looked, and behold a pale horse: and his name that sat on him was Death, and Hell followed with him. And power was given unto them over the fourth part of the earth, to kill with sword, and with hunger, and with death, and with the beasts of the earth" (Revelation 6:7-8)

It was a pale horse sent out to the earth this time when the fourth seal was opened by Lord Jesus Christ, who was the "Lamb slain" for our sake, the only one found worthy to take the scroll from the LORD Jehovah, who sat on the throne. He was the only one worthy to open the seven seals of the scroll. All power was given by the LORD Jehovah to Lord Jesus Christ, the Son of God, who is the express image of the Father. The LORD, who sat on the throne, lives forever and ever.

When the fourth seal was opened there was heard the voice of the fourth living creature, who proclaimed that a pale horse went out to the earth, and the name of the rider on the horse was Death; and Hell followed death. The fourth living creature had the face of an eagle, indicative of the power Lord Jesus Christ wields in the universe and on every living being. The voice of the living creature proclaimed that all power was given by God to the rider on the pale horse to kill fourth part of the earth, and with hunger and death, and with the beasts of the earth.

Man was disobedient from the beginning and every time he transgressed the commandments of God he was chastened. When it came to the disobedience of His chosen people, the children of Israel He was very stern in His chastisement and did not spare even Jerusalem.

Some of the glaring instances of disobedience by the children of Israel were mentioned in Ezekiel Chapter 14.

The LORD was very stern in his warning and asked prophet Ezekiel as to whether the LORD should be consulted by the elders for lenience toward their forward behavior in resorting to idol-worship; nay. The LORD said if anyone of the house of Israel took idols into one's heart and worshipped them the LORD would chastise them according to the multitude of their idols.

"For thus saith the Lord GOD; How much more when I send my four sore judgments upon Jerusalem, the sword, and the famine, and the noisome beast, and the pestilence, to cut off from it man and beast?" (Ezekiel 14:21)

Lord Jesus Christ was their Messiah and yet they rejected Him. It will be in the future that they realize after facing "great tribulation" that He was their Messiah. Jesus said:

"O Jerusalem, Jerusalem, thou that killest the prophets, and stonest them which are sent unto thee, how often would I have gathered thy children together, even as a hen gathereth her chickens under her wings, and ye would not!" (Matthew 23:37)

"For then shall be great tribulation, such as was not since the beginning of the world to this time, no, nor ever shall be" (Matthew 24:21)

The unleashing of the power of God on the earth and earth-dwellers, in future, will be because in due season when it was appropriate for them to accept Lord Jesus Christ as their Messiah, they neglected Him and salvation. Jews and Gentiles, all alike, crucified Jesus on the cross thinking that by doing so, they were going to be winners but alas! It was not so. Their actions helped the purposes of God being fulfilled. It pleased the Father to bruise Him on the cross in order that He could become propitiation for us and whosoever confesses that Jesus as Lord, and believes in heart that God raised from the dead will receive salvation.

Lord Jesus Christ said all power is given to Him and He holds the power to the Death and Hades. After the "great white throne" Judgment the death and hell will be cast into the "lake of fire" along with those whose names were not found in the "book of life".

"And I saw a great white throne, and him that sat on it, from whose face the earth and the heaven fled away; and there was found no place for them. And I saw the dead, small and great, stand before God; and the books were opened: and another book was opened, which is the book of life: and the dead were judged out of those things which were written in the books, according to their works. And the sea gave up the dead which were in it; and death and hell delivered up the dead which were in them: and they were judged every man according to their works. And death and hell were cast into the lake of fire. This is the second death. And whosoever was not found written in the book of life was cast into the lake of fire" (Revelation 20:11-15)

There is provision to escape from the "great tribulation". The word of God says...

"That if thou shalt confess with thy mouth the Lord Jesus, and shalt believe in thine heart that God hath raised him from the dead, thou shalt be saved" (Romans 10:9)

CHAPTER 16
FIFTH SEAL OPENED

(From Revelation 6:9-11)

"When he opened the fifth seal, I saw under the altar the souls of those who had been slain for the word of God and for the witness they had borne. They cried out with a loud voice, "O Sovereign Lord, holy and true, how long before you will judge and avenge our blood on those who dwell on the earth?" Then they were each given a white robe and told to rest a little longer, until the number of their fellow servants and their brothers should be complete, who were to be killed as they themselves had been" (Revelation 6:9-11 ESV)

A notable feature that needs our cognizance is that when the fifth seal is opened there was no announcement from any of the four living creatures of the impending events that would come to pass. Instead, John saw the souls of those saints who were persecuted and killed for the word of God and bearing witness for the Lord.

The souls of those killed for standing for the Lord may have been there under the altar for quite a great deal of time. However, they knew that the Lord would avenge their blood on those who dwell on the earth, but did not know how long it would take. Rather, in their impatience they seek an answer from the Sovereign Lord.

The Lord said to them that they should wait until the number of martyrs for Him is complete with those fellow servants and their brothers who would die, just as they were persecuted and killed. Each soul under the altar was given a white robe. The answer is found in Revelation 7:14 where one of the elders said they, and the rest of the ones killed later as martyrs for the Lord, during "great tribulation", came out and had "washed their robes, and made them white in the blood of the Lamb"

It is but natural for human beings to cry to the Lord, when their enemies are still in good life enjoying the pleasures of life. When Psalmist was in much agony he cried to the LORD this way several times.

The cry of the souls, which are under the altar, to the Lord was similar. They sought vengeance by the Lord, as soon as possible, not knowing God's purposes.

"O Lord, how long shall the wicked, how long shall the wicked exult?" Psalm 94:3

"How long, O Lord? Will you hide yourself forever? How long will your wrath burn like fire?" Psalm 89:46

The souls under the altar were of those who stood for the Lord during "great tribulation" and had neither worshipped Antichrist or his image nor received the "mark of the beast" on their foreheads or their hands. They came to life with Christ to reign with Him for a thousand years.

"Then I saw thrones, and seated on them were those to whom the authority to judge was committed. Also I saw the souls of those who had been beheaded for the testimony of Jesus and for the word of God, and those who had not worshiped the beast or its image and had not received its mark on their foreheads or their hands. They came to life and reigned with Christ for a thousand years" (Revelation 20:4

There are few interesting points to take note of. The souls were under the altar. The temple was already destroyed in AD 70, before John wrote Revelation in about AD 96, and therefore, this is surely a vision, alluding to the brazen altar, where the sacrifices and prayers were offered by priests, and which was outside the Tabernacle, or Temple of God.

The other altar, where the incense was burnt and prayers were offered by the high priest, was the golden altar, which was in the Holy place.

The souls under the altar referred to here, were alive and conscious talking to the Lord and, therefore, the scene is in heaven. These souls had white robes given to them signifying that they were saved from their sins, and were righteous before God.

It also shows that the souls do not die or lose conscience or cease to exist when man dies. The souls were alive, seeking a quick avenge of their blood shed by the earth-dwellers. However, they were told that the Lord knows the appropriate time to avenge their blood and surely He does so in due season.

In Matthew 19:28 Jesus said to His disciples that in the new world, when He sits on His glorious throne, they will also sit on their twelve thrones and judge the twelve tribes of Israel. This judgment refers to "the judgment seat of Christ" where rewards are given. Daniel prophesied about this judgment.

 "As I looked, thrones were placed, and the Ancient of Days took his seat; his clothing was white as snow, and the hair of his head like pure wool; his throne was fiery flames; its wheels were burning fire" Daniel 7:9

"For the Son of man shall come in the glory of his Father with his angels; and then he shall reward every man according to his works" (Matthew 16:27)

CHAPTER 17
SIXTH SEAL OPENED

(From Revelation 6:12-17)

"And I beheld when he had opened the sixth seal, and, lo, there was a great earthquake; and the sun became black as sackcloth of hair, and the moon became as blood; And the stars of heaven fell unto the earth, even as a fig tree casteth her untimely figs, when she is shaken of a mighty wind. And the heaven departed as a scroll when it is rolled together; and every mountain and island were moved out of their places. And the kings of the earth, and the great men, and the rich men, and the chief captains, and the mighty men, and every bondman, and every free man, hid themselves in the dens and in the rocks of the mountains; And said to the mountains and rocks, Fall on us, and hide us from the face of him that sitteth on the throne, and from the wrath of the Lamb: For the great day of his wrath is come; and who shall be able to stand?" (Revelation 6:12-17)

In the beginning God created the heavens and the earth. God brought light into existence by His word and He separated light from the darkness on the first day. Thereafter, on the fourth day, He made two great lights, one to rule by day and another to rule by night, and set them in the firmament of the heaven for signs, and for seasons, and for days, and years (cf. Genesis 1:1-14)

Notice even before the two greater lights, which God set them in the firmament of the heaven to rule by day and night, there was light, which He separated from darkness. The greater lights that are identified by us "sun" and "moon" were set in the firmament of heaven, for man to identify signs, seasons, days, and years. He also created stars of the heavens, which after their assigned time will fall off to the ground from their places, at as much ease as figs fall from fig tree when the tree is shaken by mighty wind.

Fig trees have during winter season figs that are not ripe under its leaves, and they hang on until spring season. However, when violent wind shakes the tree it casts them off to the ground with great ease. The comparison is made to show with what ease God will shake off the stars from off their places to the earth.

No surprise Jesus cursed fig tree when He was hungry and looked for figs in out of season to see if there were any on the tree, but when He found nothing but leaves he cursed it, and it withered out instantly (cf. Mark 11:13)

Satan, who is called "the prince of the power of the air" (in Ephesians 2:2; 6:12) will be cast off along with stars and the sun is darkened and the moon loses its light when the "Son of man" comes in the clouds great power and glory (cf. Mark 13:24-26)

Apostle Peter, who was disciple of Lord Jesus Christ, gives us vital information in his second epistle about second coming of Lord Jesus Christ. He says in the last days scoffers, walking after their own lusts, will question as to where the promise of the coming of Jesus was. They would say their fathers were dead, and everything continues as it was from the beginning of the creation. They willingly ignore the fact that the earth is standing out of the water and in the water. They ignore the fact that during Noah's days the earth was submerged under water and all but Noah's family perished.

The Lord is not slack in his promise but He is longsuffering towards us and His delay is because He does not want anyone to perish. He says "... one day is with the Lord as a thousand years, and a thousand years as one day".

The day of the Lord comes as a thief in the night and according to Lord's will, the heavens shall pass away with great noise, and the elements will burn with fervent heat, the earth and all the works therein will be burned up. Nonetheless, God creates New Heavens and New Earth wherein there will be righteousness. It is in the New Heavens and in the New Earth that His followers will live in eternity. (Cf. 2 Peter 3:3-18)

"For, behold, I create new heavens and a new earth: and the former shall not be remembered, nor come into mind" (Isaiah 65:17)

Now, when the sixth seal was opened in heaven by Lord Jesus Christ, there was earthquake, and the sun became black as sackcloth of hair, and the moon became as blood; and the stars of heaven fell unto the earth.

Heavens that were created in the beginning will roll up like scroll and depart. Every mountain and island will move out of their places. The unbelievers, whether they are kings of the earth, or great men, or rich men or chief captains in authority, or mighty men, or bondmen, or freeman; they will all hide in dens and in the rocks of the mountains to escape from the wrath of Lord Jesus Christ, whom they have not accepted as Savior. They will still see the light that was created in the beginning and cry to the mountains to fall upon them and hide from the LORD, who is on the throne, and from the wrath of the Lamb.

It is the great day of the wrath that was to come, and none will be able to face it. The heavens, and the earth that we see now, are reserved unto fire until the Day of Judgment. The ungodly are destined to destruction (cf. 2 Peter 3:7).

There is comfort for the children of Israel that they will be saved when they confess that Jesus as their Messiah. They will have their land allotted to them in the New Earth as described Isaiah 65:17 to 66:22 and Ezekiel Chapter 48 and their city shall be called "Jehovah-Shammah" (cf. Jer. 3:17; 33:16; Zech. 2:10; Rev. 21:3; Rev. 22:3).

"It was round about eighteen thousand measures: and the name of the city from that day shall be, The LORD is there" (Ezekiel 48:35)

For the church there is great hope that it will not be on the earth when all these cataclysmic destructions are wrought by the Lord.

"For God hath not appointed us to wrath, but to obtain salvation by our Lord Jesus Christ" (1 Thessalonians 5:9)

It is now the time to confess that Jesus is the Lord, and believe in heart that God raised Him from the dead. God so loved the world that He sent His one and only Son Jesus into this world to take upon Himself our sin and He, who had no sin in Him, was made sin for us. Whoever believes in Him shall not perish but have everlasting life. All those who are saved will be "caught up" to meet the Lord in the air, and be with Him forever and ever. All those whose names are not found in the Lamb's book of life will be cast into the "'lake of fire".

"And death and hell were cast into the lake of fire. This is the second death. And whosoever was not found written in the book of life was cast into the lake of fire" (Revelation 20:14-15)

"And shall cast them into a furnace of fire: there shall be wailing and gnashing of teeth" (Matthew 13:42)

CHAPTER 18
THE IMPRESSIVE INTERLUDE

(FROM REVELATION CHAPTER 7)

The text from Revelation Chapter 7 is posted followed by my exposition. The original text is posted to show that I am not adding anything to the text or removing anything from the text. The explanation that follows is I understand the text.

The Text

Revelation 7:1 And after these things I saw four angels standing on the four corners of the earth, holding the four winds of the earth, that the wind should not blow on the earth, nor on the sea, nor on any tree.
2 And I saw another angel ascending from the east, having the seal of the living God: and he cried with a loud voice to the four angels, to whom it was given to hurt the earth and the sea,
3 Saying, Hurt not the earth, neither the sea, nor the trees, till we have sealed the servants of our God in their foreheads.
4 And I heard the number of them which were sealed: and there were sealed an hundred and forty and four thousand of all the tribes of the children of Israel.
5 Of the tribe of Juda were sealed twelve thousand. Of the tribe of Reuben were sealed twelve thousand. Of the tribe of Gad were sealed twelve thousand.
6 Of the tribe of Aser were sealed twelve thousand. Of the tribe of Nepthalim were sealed twelve thousand. Of the tribe of Manasses were sealed twelve thousand.
7 Of the tribe of Simeon were sealed twelve thousand. Of the tribe of Levi were sealed twelve thousand. Of the tribe of Issachar were sealed twelve thousand.

8 Of the tribe of Zabulon were sealed twelve thousand. Of the tribe of Joseph were sealed twelve thousand. Of the tribe of Benjamin were sealed twelve thousand.

9 After this I beheld, and, lo, a great multitude, which no man could number, of all nations, and kindreds, and people, and tongues, stood before the throne, and before the Lamb, clothed with white robes, and palms in their hands;

10 And cried with a loud voice, saying, Salvation to our God which sitteth upon the throne, and unto the Lamb.

11 And all the angels stood round about the throne, and about the elders and the four beasts, and fell before the throne on their faces, and worshipped God,

12 Saying, Amen: Blessing, and glory, and wisdom, and thanksgiving, and honour, and power, and might, be unto our God for ever and ever. Amen.

13 And one of the elders answered, saying unto me, What are these which are arrayed in white robes? and whence came they?

14 And I said unto him, Sir, thou knowest. And he said to me, These are they which came out of great tribulation, and have washed their robes, and made them white in the blood of the Lamb.

15 Therefore are they before the throne of God, and serve him day and night in his temple: and he that sitteth on the throne shall dwell among them.

16 They shall hunger no more, neither thirst any more; neither shall the sun light on them, nor any heat.

17 For the Lamb which is in the midst of the throne shall feed them, and shall lead them unto living fountains of waters: and God shall wipe away all tears from their eyes.

Exposition:

Revelation Chapter 7 can be identified as an interlude or break or intermission between Chapter 6 and Chapter 8. (This kind of interlude happens several times in the Book of Revelation – 6, a break and 7 like six angels, a break and seventh, six trumpets, a break and seventh).

This chapter provides us a quest to seek answers to some of our intriguing questions related to the Church, Great Tribulation, The sealing of the twelve tribes, preaching the Gospel during Great Tribulation, the Church reigning with Lord Jesus, and the worshippers in the Temple during Millennium.

Apostle John says, after the things mentioned in Chapter 6 of Revelation had come to pass, he saw four angels standing on the four corners of the earth, holding four winds that they may not hurt the earth, or the sea, or the trees before the appointed time.

The four angels were strong enough to hold the winds. The four winds blow from four poles of the earth; the North Pole, the South Pole, the East Pole, and the West Pole. Who can hold the winds except angels at the command of God? Who can direct the paths of the winds except God Himself?

Another angel came from the east and said to the angels not to hurt the earth until the servants of God were sealed in their foreheads. John heard the number of those who were sealed on their foreheads and they were 144,000; twelve thousand from each of the twelve tribes as mentioned in Revelation 7:5-8

A common question that arises in the minds of believers is that will anyone be able to be saved during great tribulation period, and if so, who are those, and how salvation is provided. The reason to ask such question is because of the knowledge that we have that the church will be 'caught up' when Lord Jesus Christ comes again and Holy Spirit, who is the restrainer, is withdrawn from the world.

Holy Spirit, the restrainer, is removed from the earth immediately when the Church is caught up and with the absence of Holy Spirit in the world, the Antichrist is revealed.

"And now ye know that which restrains, that he should be revealed in his own time"(2 Thessalonians 2:6)

Until the Church is 'caught up' the restrainer restrains Antichrist from being revealed and to have any power in the world. This Antichrist is not the one that is referred in 1 John, but he is the 'man of sin' and 'son of perdition'.

The members of the Church have glorified bodies, and will reign with Lord Jesus Christ on those who are saved during the great Tribulation period and thereafter.

"In a moment, in the twinkling of an eye, at the last trump: for the trumpet shall sound, and the dead shall be raised incorruptible, and we shall be changed" (1 Corinthians 15:52)

After the Church is 'caught up' there would be no restrainer in the world, and the evil will be rampant. The Holy Spirit visits the earth on specific individuals just as He was visiting in the Old Testament period.

In this period of interlude the 144,000 of purely Jewish descends from the twelve tribes of Israel, will be sealed unto redemption, and they will be protected from Great Tribulation. They are sealed unto redemption similar to the members of the Church are sealed inasmuch as they accept Jesus as their Savior. They come to be under the Church, where is there is no difference between Jews and Gentiles.

"In whom ye also trusted, after that ye heard the word of truth, the gospel of your salvation: in whom also after that ye believed, ye were sealed with that holy Spirit of promise" (Ephesians 1:13)

The protection they enjoy will be just as the children of Israel were protected from Egyptian plagues.

The 144,000 are those, whose eyes are not blind anymore, but opened to see and believe the truth of the knowledge of the Lord Jesus Christ. They are the ones who enjoy the same privilege as the Church enjoys.

"But their minds were made dull, for to this day the same veil remains when the old covenant is read. It has not been removed, because only in Christ is it taken away. Even to this day when Moses is read, a veil covers their hearts. 16 But whenever anyone turns to the Lord, the veil is taken away" 2 Corinthians 3:14-16.

Did God chose only 144,000 to be sealed during the great tribulation period out of 15 million Jews in the world today? Yes, that is what the text says, and no one is authorized to allegorize to some other number, or say 'Church is spiritual Israel' etc. The Church is the body of Christ and not spiritual Israel. Israel is not the Church. The rest of them are the ones who have refused to accept Jesus as their Messiah, but will acknowledge Him as their Messiah when the 144,000 preach Gospel to the world.

The Bible says every knee shall bow and acknowledge the name of Jesus and the rest of the Jews who are not sealed are no exception to this saying:

"That at the name of Jesus every knee should bow, of things in heaven, and things in earth, and things under the earth"
(Philippians 2:10)

The Church in this period will be in heaven with the Lord, and these 144,000 are sealed with the Holy Spirit unto salvation, just as any member of the Church is sealed with the Holy Spirit unto redemption to be conformed to the image of His Son.

The member of the Church does not mean a member of local Church, but the body of Christ, whose head is Lord Jesus Christ. It should be clear by now that the Church is 'caught up' when the Lord comes again with the shout of the archangel at the last trump and the dead in Christ shall rise first and those who are alive at that time will be caught to meet the Lord in the air and be with Him for ever and ever.

"For the Lord himself shall descend from heaven with a shout, with the voice of the archangel, and with the trump of God: and the dead in Christ shall rise first: Then we which are alive and remain shall be caught up together with them in the clouds, to meet the Lord in the air: and so shall we ever be with the Lord"
(1 Thessalonians 4:16-17)

Those Jewish descendants numbering 144,000 from the twelve tribes would be on the earth yet they belong to the Church. Those 144,000 will proclaim the Gospel of Jesus Christ to the ends of the earth, and at this time that the promise would be fulfilled that there shall not a single one left on this earth that has not heard the Gospel of Jesus Christ.

After 144,000 were sealed, John saw a great multitude that could not be numbered by any man coming up from all nations, all kindred, all people, and tongues. They all stood before the

Lamb. They were all clothed in white robes, and palms in their hands. They cried with loud voice saying "Salvation belongs to our God, who sits on the throne, and to the Lamb."

This multitude of people is the remnant of Jews and Gentiles saved during the Great Tribulation period by the Gospel of Jesus Christ proclaimed by 144,000, and martyred. There is a clear demarcation here and the Church has the members of Christ, and the 144,000 sealed of the Jewish descendants. They do have the glorified bodies and will worship the Lord in heaven. All the 144,000 will all be in the new Heaven.

There is no temple in heaven. This is very firmly affirmed in Revelation 21:22.

And I saw no temple therein: for the Lord God Almighty and the Lamb are the temple of it. (Revelation 21:22)

The temple that is referred to in Revelation Chapter 11:1 is one that would be built during Great Tribulation period. This is evident from the fact that the seventh trumpet was not blown nor seven vials were poured out during the time period mentioned in Revelation Chapter 11:1.

There is mention of 'temple' in Revelation Chapter 11:19. This is the actual abode of God, the Holy of Holies to which there is access for men. John saw the Ark of the Testament of God there and "there came flashes of lightning, rumblings, peals of thunder, an earthquake and a severe hailstorm". Lightning, thunders, and earthquake describe the majesty of God.

"Then God's temple in heaven was opened, and within his temple was seen the ark of his covenant. And there came flashes of lightning, rumblings, peals of thunder, an earthquake and a severe hailstorm". *(Revelation 11:19)*

And I saw no temple therein: for the Lord God Almighty and the Lamb are the temple of it. (Revelation 21:22)

These multitudes, of people that John saw, are those, who would have heard the Gospel of Jesus Christ from the mouths of 144,000 of Jewish redeemed children of God. These multitudes of people do not have the glorified bodies and they will worship the Lord in the temple on the new earth.

One of the elders inquired John if he knew who in white robes were, and where they came from. When John said "Sir, you know", the elder said to him, "These are they who have come out of the great tribulation; they have washed their robes and made them white in the blood of the Lamb".

The elder also explained to John that they are before the throne of God and serve Him day and night in His temple, and He who sits on the throne will dwell among them. Because the LORD is with them they shall neither hunger nor thirst anymore and neither the sun shall light on them nor would they suffer from any heat. The Lamb will feed them and lead them to the living fountains of waters. God will wipe away their tears from their eyes.

My tabernacle also shall be with them: yea, I will be their God, and they shall be my people. (Ezekiel 37:27)

John heard the number of those who were sealed on their foreheads and they were 144,000; twelve thousand from each of the twelve tribes as mentioned in Revelation 7:5-8.

Those who were sealed were

From the tribe of Judah 12,000,
From the tribe of Reuben 12,000,
From the tribe of Gad 12,000,
 From the tribe of Asher 12,000,
From the tribe of Naphtali 12,000,
From the tribe of Manasseh 12,000,
 From the tribe of Simeon 12,000,
From the tribe of Levi 12,000,
From the tribe of Issachar 12,000,
 From the tribe of Zebulun 12,000,
From the tribe of Joseph 12,000, and
From the tribe of Benjamin are sealed 12,000.

Judah is listed first because Reuben lost his birthright because he defiled the bed of his father, Jacob.

The scepter is given to Judah, and Jesus is called the lion of the tribe of Judah and the scepter of Judah shall not depart from him.

Every one of the angels, who stood around the throne of God, and around the elders, and around the four beasts, fell prostrate on their faces before the throne and worshipped God saying, "Amen: Blessing, and glory, and wisdom, and thanksgiving, and honour, and power, and might, be unto our God for ever and ever. Amen".

Tribulation Saints

In response to the Gospel message proclaimed by the 144,000 Jews, who were sealed from the twelve tribes of Israel, there was a multitude of people accepted Jesus as the Lord, and John could not number them. They were from every nation, every tribe, and people and languages. They were all standing before the throne and the Lamb. What then, is the difference between the throne and the Lamb? Obviously The Father God was in His throne, still invisible for anyone, and the Lamb of God, who is our Savior, Lord Jesus Christ was by His side.

The multitude, who could not be numbered, cried out in a loud voice saying:

"Salvation belongs to our God,
who sits on the throne,
and to the Lamb"

The angels, who were standing around the throne, and around the elders and four living creatures, fell prostrate down before the throne and worshipped God saying:

"Amen!
Praise and glory
and wisdom and thanks and honor
and power and strength
be to our God for ever and ever.
Amen!"

While the multitude worshipped saying "Salvation belongs to our God, who sits on the throne, and to the Lamb" the angels worshipped God saying: "Amen, praise and glory and wisdom and thanks and honor, and power and strength be to our God for ever and ever. Amen.

From among the twenty four elders, who were representatives of the Church, one elder asked John if he recognized those multitudes that were in white robes, and where they came from.

As it was a rhetorical question designed to answer rather than seeking an answer, John said to the elder "Sir, you know". If there were disciples of Jesus or anyone from either Old Testament saints viz. Abraham, Isaac, or Jacob, or New Testament saints, John would have certainly recognized them, but he did not recognize anyone of them; rather he said, "Sir, you know".

The elder answered John that they are the ones who have not obeyed or worshipped Antichrist and come out of great tribulation having become martyrs for Lord Jesus Christ and rose to life.

A very notable fact here is that they are ever before the throne of God and serve Him day and night in His temple. The question is how the temple appeared in heaven. The answer is that the temple is not in new heaven, but is on the new earth, and God is in His holy temple, for them, as promised in Jeremiah 31:33 and Ezekiel Chapter 37:28. God made covenant as follows:

"This is the covenant I will make with the people of Israel after that time," declares the Lord. "I will put my law in their minds and write it on their hearts. I will be their God, and they will be my people" Jeremiah 31:33

For New Testament believers it was already fulfilled according to Luke 22:20.

"In the same way, after the supper he took the cup, saying, "This cup is the new covenant in my blood, which is poured out for you".

The multitude that came out from the great tribulation served God in his temple. God will shelter them with His presence, and they never again thirst, not does sun will beat them down and no scorching heat will hurt them. The Lamb at the center of the throne will be their shepherd, and he will lead them to springs of living water, and God will wipe away tears from their eyes.

The prophecy in Isaiah 49:10 will be fulfilled.

"They will neither hunger nor thirst,
     nor will the desert heat or the sun beat down on them.
He who has compassion on them will guide them
     and lead them beside springs of water"

CHAPTER 19
SEVENTH SEAL OPENED

(From Revelation chapter 8:1-11)

(The Seventh Seal and the Golden Censer)

"When the Lamb opened the seventh seal, there was silence in heaven for about half an hour. Then I saw the seven angels who stand before God, and seven trumpets were given to them" (Revelation 8:1-2 ESV)

There was an interlude between openings of the sixth seal and the seventh and happenings during that period are detailed in Revelation Chapter 7. With the opening of the seventh seal in Revelation Chapter 8 a new series of catastrophic events begin. These are not included in the first four seals already open but separate events that occur in addition to them.

There was half an hour silence when Lord Jesus Christ opened seventh seal. No conjecture can be made as to what that silence was for. After the expiry of that silence there was seen by John the Apostle, seven angels who stood before the God and they were given seven trumpets to blow.

In addition there was another angel, who came with golden censer, stood at the altar. It is not possible to say who this angel was, as there are varied opinions about him. Some believe that he was an angel appointed to execute that particular service at that point of time; but that does not hold good ground because there is no other mediator between man and God except Lord Jesus Christ.

This causes us to take our memories back to the period of Moses when the LORD commanded him to build Tabernacle for Him. The model of the Tabernacle is the shadow of the sanctuary in heaven. It was in the Tabernacle, where the high priest stood with golden censer and offered incense.

The incense is burnt at the golden altar in the Tabernacle to offer the prayers of the children of Israel to the LORD. After offering the prayers the high priest entered the "most holy" place where the LORD spoke to him. The LORD's Shekinah glory came and spoke to the high priest from the "mercy seat", which was upon the "ark of the testimony", guarded by two cherubims facing one opposite to another with their wings stretched forth high on the "ark of the testimony" (Ref. Exodus 25:20)

High Priests of Aaronic order were only authorized by God to enter into the "holy place" and "most holy" Place in the Tabernacle. Cf. Exodus 30:1, 7, 34-38; Leviticus 16:2; Leviticus 16:12-13)

This also reminds about Zechariah who stood before the Lord to offer incense in the order of his course, according to the custom of the priesthood, angel Gabriel appeared to him to announce that his wife Elizabeth shall bear him a son, whose name shall be John.

The writer of Hebrews writes in Hebrews 1:3 that Lord Jesus Christ, who being the brightness of the glory of the Father, and the express image of His person, who by upholding all things by the word of His power, when He had by Himself purged our sins, sat down on the right hand of the Majesty on high. He is our High Priest, having become propitiation for us and offered Himself as sacrifice for our sake on the cross.

"Who being the brightness of his glory, and the express image of his person, and upholding all things by the word of his power, when he had by himself purged our sins, sat down on the right hand of the Majesty on high" (Hebrews 1:3)

"He has no need, like those high priests, to offer sacrifices daily, first for his own sins and then for those of the people, since he did this once for all when he offered up himself" (Hebrews 7:27 ESV)

"And for this cause he is the mediator of the new testament, that by means of death, for the redemption of the transgressions that were under the first testament, they which are called might receive the promise of eternal inheritance" (Hebrews 9:15)

Jesus is not an angel; but in the Old Testament period Jesus appeared as the "angel of the LORD" visible to the man for a small duration of time until the purpose of the LORD was complete (It is called "Theophany": Examples are found in Genesis 16:11; Genesis 22:11 Exodus 3:2 etc.) The angels do not accept worship (Matt. 4:10; Rev. 19:10; Rev. 22:8-9 etc.).

Even though here in the context it is not specifically mentioned as "angel of the LORD", yet the responsibility He was holding as mediator to stand at the altar, having golden censer, with much incense to offer the prayers of all saints upon the golden altar which was before the throne, gives us enough evidence for us to believe that He was none other than Jesus Christ. (Ref. Revelation 8:3-4). These prayers could be of those tribulation martyred saints, who were under the altar as we read in Revelation 6:9, seeking avenging of their blood.

In due time when the church is to be separated from the wrath of God, and the "Restrainer" is taken out the way, the "man of sin", who is the "son of perdition" will be revealed. However, let no man be deceived because that day shall not come unless apostasy comes first (cf. 2 Thessalonians 2:3-7)

To begin with, the wrath of God in the last days comes upon only on the earth and the earth-dwellers, after the church is removed from this earth. Lord Jesus Christ, who alone is worthy to open the scroll, will open the seven seals of the scroll, one after another. Each seal, when opened brings forth unique catastrophic consequence on the earth. The Church, which is the body of Christ, is protected from the wrath of God and, as Jesus said, the gates of hell shall not prevail against it (cf. Matt 16:18).

Whether one calls protection of the Church as "rapture" or "caught up" or moving away to be with the Lord, who comes in clouds in the air, etc., the purpose aimed is to protect the church from the wrath of God.

The wrath of God is visibly seen in its rigorous form in the last phase of 3 ½ years of the seventieth week; nevertheless, its commencement is at the beginning of the seven year period (which is the 70th week of Daniel's 70-week prophecy)

CHAPTER 20
FIRST TRUMPET BLOWN

(From Revelation chapter 8:1-11)

"The first angel blew his trumpet, and there followed hail and fire, mixed with blood, and these were thrown upon the earth. And a third of the earth was burned up, and a third of the trees were burned up, and all green grass was burned up" (Revelation 8:7 ESV)

As seen by John in his vision, about the future events, the seven angels start blowing their respective trumpets after the silence for half an hour was over. When the first trumpet was sounded by the first angel, hail and fire mixed with blood were blown upon the earth and as a consequence it the third of the earth was burned up, and a third of the trees were burned up and all the grass was burned up.

In all the cases, where hail was mentioned in scriptures, the reference is made to punishment from God (cf. Job 38:22-23; Psalm 18:13; Haggai 2:17; Isaiah 30:30; Ezekiel 13:11). A very glaring example is seen in the case of Egyptians who suffered hail and fire under Pharaoh in consequence of his refusal to release the children of Israel from the slavery of bondage.

Moses demanded Pharaoh, at the commandment of the LORD, to release the children of Israel from the bondage of slavery in Egypt but Pharaoh refused to release them. One of the ten plagues God wrought upon Pharaoh and Egypt was hail and fire. Moses stretched forth the rod in his hand "toward heaven and the LORD sent thunder and hail and fire ran upon the ground". Hail mingled with fire was very intense, such as there was none like it before, in all the land of Egypt. Hail smote everything that was in the field, both man and beast and broke every tree of the field. However, in the land of Goshen, where the children of Israel lived there was no hail (cf. Exodus 9:23-26).

It is time now for those who have not confessed that Jesus is Lord, to do so now, and believe in heart that God raised Him from the dead. The Bible says they will, otherwise, enter into tribulation period. Every knee shall bow to Him and every tongue shall confess to God that He is the Lord (cf. Romans 14:11; Isaiah 45:23; Philippians 2:10)

"Have this mind among yourselves, which is yours in Christ Jesus, who, though he was in the form of God, did not count equality with God a thing to be grasped, but emptied himself, by taking the form of a servant, being born in the likeness of men. And being found in human form, he humbled himself by becoming obedient to the point of death, even death on a cross. Therefore God has highly exalted him and bestowed on him the name that is above every name, so that at the name of Jesus every knee should bow, in heaven and on earth and under the earth, and every tongue confess that Jesus Christ is Lord, to the glory of God the Father" (Philippians 2:5-11 ESV)

CHAPTER 21
SECOND TRUMPET BLOWN

(From Revelation Chapter 8:8-9)

"And the second angel sounded, and as it were a great mountain burning with fire was cast into the sea: and the third part of the sea became blood; And the third part of the creatures which were in the sea, and had life, died; and the third part of the ships were destroyed" (Revelation 8:8-9)

There were four catastrophic events seen when the second angel blew the second trumpet.

1. as it were a great mountain burning with fire was cast into the sea
2. and the third part of the sea became blood
3. And the third part of the creatures which were in the sea, and had life, died
4. and the third part of the ships were destroyed

The first few references that we see about the mountain that is referred to here are of Noah's family and his sons and their wives who went out of the ark after the flood receded. The original name of the central district of Armenia was Ararat, where the Noah's ark rested in the seventh month, on the seventeenth day of the month upon its mountain (cf. Genesis 8:4).

The posterity of Noah's family, and those of his sons and his wives, journeyed from the east and "they found a plain in the land of Shinar and dwelt there" (cf. Genesis 11:2). This was one hundred and thirty days after the flood, and this place was later called "Chaldees", which was renamed later as "Assyria".

God blessed Noah and his sons and said to them "…Be fruitful, and multiply, and replenish the earth" (Genesis 9:1). However, the posterity of Noah violated God's command.

"Then they said, 'Come, let us build ourselves a city and a tower with its top in the heavens, and let us make a name for ourselves, lest we be dispersed over the face of the whole earth.' " (Genesis 11:4 ESV)

As they were building the city and tower that they thought would reach the heaven, the LORD came down to see the city and the tower that they were building. The LORD Said "Behold, they are one people, and they have all one language, and this is only the beginning of what they will do. And nothing that they propose to do will now be impossible for them. Come, let us go down and there confuse their language, so that they may not understand one another's speech."

"Therefore is the name of it called Babel; because the LORD did there confound the language of all the earth: and from thence did the LORD scatter them abroad upon the face of all the earth" (Genesis 11:9)

This is the very mountain referred to in Revelation 8:8; 18:8, 9 and it is in Babylon. The LORD was against it from since the time human government at Babel tried to overthrow God's plans. The LORD cursed the mountain by saying:

"Behold, I am against you, O destroying mountain, declares the LORD, which destroys the whole earth; I will stretch out my hand against you, and roll you down from the crags, and make you a burnt mountain" (Jeremiah 51:25 ESV)

"O you who dwell by many waters, rich in treasures, your end has come; the thread of your life is cut"
(Jeremiah 51:13 ESV)

"And upon her forehead was a name written, MYSTERY, BABYLON THE GREAT, THE MOTHER OF HARLOTS AND ABOMINATIONS OF THE EARTH" (Revelation 17:5)

"This is what the Lord GOD showed me: behold, the Lord GOD was calling for a judgment by fire, and it devoured the great deep and was eating up the land" (Amos 7:4 ESV)

John in his vision saw the future catastrophic event. He saw the second angel blowing the second trumpet and then something like a great mountain burning with fire was thrown into the sea; consequently, a third of the sea became blood. A third of the living creatures in the sea died and a third of the ships were destroyed.

In consequence of the seven trumpets blown by the seven angels immense is damage is caused to the earth, mountains, plantation, earth-dwellers, and the seas. God's wrath is so intense that it causes total destruction of the original creation and un-creation begins.

Citing from Psalm 24:1 Apostle Paul wrote that the earth is the Lord's and the fullness thereof (Ref. 1 Corinthians 10:26); but this statement was made as if to issue a clarification about eating the food that is offered to idols. The sin on this earth and the worldly pleasures are still controlled by Satan. The church will be separated from the evil that is on this earth when Lord

Jesus Christ comes in clouds as written in 1 Thessalonians 4:16-17.

During the seven-year period of Daniel's prophesied seventieth week there will be gradual gathering of those who believe in the LORD when the gospel is preached by 144,000. This is the time when the preaching of the Gospel will reach to the ends of the earth and everyone on earth will hear about Lord Jesus Christ.

After total un-creation, there will come into existence the new heavens and the new earth that the LORD would have created by then. The prophecy in Isaiah 65:17 is not yet fulfilled and it will not go unfulfilled. The church will be in the new heavens and those who are saved after the church is "caught up" and during the "Sheep and Goat Judgment" will be on the new earth. Thus the church, which has Jews and Gentiles in it, has the privilege to be greater than the Israel.

"For, behold, I create new heavens and a new earth: and the former shall not be remembered, nor come into mind" (Isaiah 65:17)

CHAPTER 22
THIRD TRUMPET BLOWN

(From Revelation 8:10-11)

"The third angel blew his trumpet, and a great star fell from heaven, blazing like a torch, and it fell on a third of the rivers and on the springs of water. The name of the star is Wormwood. A third of the waters became wormwood, and many people died from the water, because it had been made bitter" (Revelation 8:10-11 ESV)

When the third trumpet was blown by the third angel a great star fell. It did not fall like a dead or gruesome or horrible meteor, but like a bright blazing torch and its name was "Wormwood". This star's name is derived from a plant named "wormwood" from which bitter and poisonous juice is extracted.

The first usage of this word "wormwood" was in Deuteronomy 29:18, where the LORD said to Moses to speak to the children of Israel that they should remember how the LORD redeemed them from the bondage of slavery in Egypt. He warned them that no one from among them should turn one's heart away from the Him to serve the other gods; lest there should come out from their heart bitterness and poison (cf. Deuteronomy 29:18)

Likewise, in all the following verses the word "wormwood" is used to refer bitterness in taste and poisonous in effect.

Deut. 29:18; Proverbs 5:4; Jeremiah 9:15; 23:15; Lamentations 3:15, 19; Amos 5:7 and Rev. 8:11

The sun, moon and the stars represent government and sun getting darkened, or moon losing its light, or stars falling show that the government is falling. Here the kingdom of devil starts falling apart slowly but surely.

After the "Restrainer" is moved out of the way Antichrist is revealed, who after his 3 ½ years reign breaks his promise and causes "abomination of desolation". This "man of sin" who is "the son of perdition" sets himself as God in the temple of God and forces people to worship him.

Whoever worships him will have "mark of the beast". Satan and the false prophet and they that worshipped his image and received the "mark of the beast" will all be cast into the "lake of fire" (cf. Rev. 16:2; Rev. 19:20; Rev. 20:12)

"And the beast was taken, and with him the false prophet that wrought miracles before him, with which he deceived them that had received the mark of the beast, and them that worshipped his image. These both were cast alive into a lake of fire burning with brimstone" (Revelation 19:20)

When this star called "wormwood" fell on a third of the rivers and on the springs of water, a terrible cataclysmic upheaval takes place. It turns a third of the fresh waters of the rivers and of the springs into bitter and poisonous and many people drink that water and die.

The time and date of Lord Jesus coming again is not known to anyone. If someone is not a part of the church to be 'caught up' to be with the Lord, he will be on this earth to face all these calamities.

When we were dead in trespasses, Christ died for us in due time and we, who were enemies to God, are given opportunity to believe in Him. This is an apt time to repent of sins and confess that Jesus is "Lord" and believe in heart that God raised Him from the dead. Whoever believes in Him will be saved and will have everlasting life.

"For the wages of sin is death; but the gift of God is eternal life through Jesus Christ our Lord" (Romans 6:23)

CHAPTER 23
FOURTH TRUMPET BLOWN

(From Revelation 8:12-13)

"And the fourth angel sounded, and the third part of the sun was smitten, and the third part of the moon, and the third part of the stars; so as the third part of them was darkened, and the day shone not for a third part of it, and the night likewise" (Revelation 8:12)

There is evidence here that the kingdom of devil will be gradually falling apart with the smiting of third part of the sun, the third part of the moon, and the third part of the stars when the fourth angel sounds the fourth trumpet. As seen by John in his vision, when the third part of the sun, moon and the stars were smitten there was no light on the third part of the earth; that is to say there was darkness on the third part of the earth. The sun was shining and the moon gave its light from the rest of their parts.

The destruction of this sinful earth is gradual and it will be complete when the Lord humbles the first creation fully to its knees. The Lord, the seed of David, will be triumphant in all His battles against the wicked earth. The heavens and the earth will fly away from His presence when He sits on the "great white throne.

"And I saw a great white throne, and him that sat on it, from whose face the earth and the heaven fled away; and there was found no place for them" (Revelation 20:11)

In the ninth plague when darkness was brought upon Egyptians they felt the seriousness of sun getting darkened for a season when Pharaoh refused to release the children of Israel from their slavery. Even as Egyptians were suffering during the period when Moses stretched out his rod at the command of the LORD and the darkness existed in the place where they lived, the children of Israel were protected.

"Then the Lord said to Moses, "Stretch out your hand toward heaven, that there may be darkness over the land of Egypt, a darkness to be felt." So Moses stretched out his hand toward heaven, and there was pitch darkness in all the land of Egypt three days. They did not see one another, nor did anyone rise from his place for three days, but all the people of Israel had light where they lived" Exodus 10:21-23

Isaiah the prophet spoke the word of the LORD in prophecy about the end time destruction.

"For the stars of the heavens and their constellations will not give their light; the sun will be dark at its rising, and the moon will not shed its light" Isaiah 13:10

"Therefore I will shake the heavens, and the earth shall remove out of her place, in the wrath of the LORD of hosts, and in the day of his fierce anger" (Isaiah 13:13)

However, during the period of thousand-year-reign by Lord Jesus Christ those who obeyed the Lord will have greater blessings bestowed on them as prophesied in Isaiah 30:26

"Moreover, the light of the moon will be as the light of the sun, and the light of the sun will be sevenfold, as the light of seven days, in the day when the Lord binds up the brokenness of his people, and heals the wounds inflicted by his blow".

After the release of the children of Israel from the bondage of slavery they reached the Red Sea and they were sore afraid but the LORD protected them by bringing darkness between them and the Egyptians in order that they may walk on the dry ground in the midst of the Red Sea; but the chasing Pharaoh, his armies and the chariots drowned in the Red sea. The LORD punishes the enemies of his children and He protects His children.

"And when they cried unto the LORD, he put darkness between you and the Egyptians, and brought the sea upon them, and covered them; and your eyes have seen what I have done in Egypt: and ye dwelt in the wilderness a long season" (Joshua 24:7)

God's mercy towards them that love Him is extremely great; but His wrath towards those who are disobedient to Him is double in its intensity than His love towards them that follow Him. That is the reason why God does not want anyone to perish. Now is the time to accept Jesus as Lord and believe in heart that God raised Him from the dead.

"For God so loved the world, that he gave his only begotten Son, that whosoever believeth in him should not perish, but have everlasting life" (John 3:16)

The sun was darkened for three hours when our sin was judged at the cross when it pleased the Father to bruise His one and only son on the cross in order that we may have everlasting life and enjoy His blessings bountifully.

"Now from the sixth hour there was darkness over all the land unto the ninth hour. And about the ninth hour Jesus cried with a loud voice, saying, Eli, Eli, lama sabachthani? that is to say, My God, my God, why hast thou forsaken me?" (Matthew 27:45-46)

During the "great tribulation" period when the wrath of God will be poured out the consequences will be very serious. The third of the sun will be darkened, the third of the moon will be darkened, and the third of the stars will be darkened. It will not be complete destruction at a stretch, but will be gradual. This could be to grant an additional time for people to come to the Lord.

After this, John saw in his vision an angel flying through the midst of heaven proclaiming to the inhabitants of the earth three "woes" when the remaining three trumpets will be sounded by the fifth, sixth and the seventh angel that bring greater destruction than that was brought when the four trumpets were blown already.

"And I beheld, and heard an angel flying through the midst of heaven, saying with a loud voice, Woe, woe, woe, to the inhabiters of the earth by reason of the other voices of the trumpet of the three angels, which are yet to sound!" (Revelation 8:13)

CHAPTER 24
FIFTH TRUMPET BLOWN

(From Revelation 9:1-12)

"And the fifth angel sounded, and I saw a star fall from heaven unto the earth: and to him was given the key of the bottomless pit" (Revelation 9:1)

"Then I looked, and I heard an eagle crying with a loud voice as it flew directly overhead, "Woe, woe, woe to those who dwell on the earth, at the blasts of the other trumpets that the three angels are about to blow!" (Revelation 8:13 ESV)

After four trumpets were blown by the four angels an eagle crying with a loud voice announced, as seen by John in his vision, there were three "Woes" to come shortly when fifth angel, sixth angel and the seventh angel will blow their respective trumpets.

None of the consequences that came about as a result of the first four angels blowing their trumpets harmed men directly; but now when the fifth angel sounded his trumpet the results were aghast and the catastrophe hurt men directly. They were not given power to harm grass of the earth or green plant or any tree.

The star that fell from the heaven to the earth had the key to the bottomless pit and its name in Hebrew was "Abaddon" and in Greek by the name "Apollyon" which means "destruction" and "destroyer" respectively. This star was an angel, which had the power to open the shaft to the bottomless pit, and he had the authority like that of a king over the creatures that came out from the bottomless pit. These creatures were locusts that had an appearance which none of us have ever seen. Catastrophic events occurring upon the earth as a result of God's wrath were prophesied by Joel the prophet.

"The appearance of them is as the appearance of horses; and as horsemen, so shall they run. Like the noise of chariots on the tops of mountains shall they leap, like the noise of a flame of fire that devoureth the stubble, as a strong people set in battle array" (Joel 2:4-5)

The creatures that came out from the bottomless pit through the shaft were peculiar ones. Thick smoke rose from the shaft as from great furnace and from it came out these locusts when "Apollyon", which had the power to open the shaft, opened it.

These locusts were neither symbolic nor imaginary but real ones whom no one has ever seen before. They had faces like human beings and crowns of gold on their head. They were like horses ready as if they were going for battle. Their hair was like women's hair and their teeth were like lion's teeth. They had breastplates of iron to cover their chests. The noise produced by their wings when they fly was like many chariots with horses rushing into battle.

They had tails and stings like scorpions; but their power to hurt was in their tails. They were authorized to hurt only for five months those who do not have the seal of God. The pain caused by the tails of these locusts is like that of pain that is caused by the sting of scorpion. They cannot and do not harm any one of the 144,000 Jewish descendants, who were sealed for redemption. (cf. Rev. 7:2, 3)

In the eighth plague that God brought forth upon Pharaoh and his people in Egypt, for not letting the children of Israel go, Moses stretches his hand, in obedience to the LORD's command, over the land of Egypt for the locusts to come upon Egypt and eat every herb of the remnant of the seventh plague of hail. (cf. Exodus 10:12) They were great in number and they rested in all the coasts of Egypt. The plague was exceedingly great and terrifying. The earth in Egypt became black as swarm of locusts covered it. They ate every herb of the land, every fruit of the tree left-behind after the plague of hail was withdrawn. No green thing of the herbs of the field could be seen in the entire region of Egypt.

Pharaoh could not bear the plague of locusts and called for Moses and Aaron in haste, and repented before them saying he sinned against the LORD their God, and against them. He prayed for mercy and forgiveness and requested them to intercede on his behalf him and his people to God and move away the impending death.

Moses went out from the presence of Pharaoh and interceded with the LORD on behalf of them and the LORD heard his prayer. The powerful hand of the LORD was seen there when He turned a mighty strong west wind that took away the locusts and removed every one of them and threw every single locust in the Red sea from the land of Egypt in answer to the intercessory prayer of Moses.

The devastation that the locusts bring forth during "great tribulation" is different in its intensity. They do not hurt the grass of the ground, but hurt only those who are not sealed by God. Those who are sealed by God are protected from the locusts but those who are not sealed by God will face His wrath.

In those days people will seek death but the death flees from them; they will not find the death.

With this the first "wow" passes off and there are two more "woes" yet to come.

CHAPTER 25
SIXTH TRUMPET BLOWN

(From Revelation Chapter 9:13-21)

"And the sixth angel sounded, and I heard a voice from the four horns of the golden altar which is before God, Saying to the sixth angel which had the trumpet, Loose the four angels which are bound in the great river Euphrates" (Revelation 9:13-14)

The golden altar in the Tabernacle was inside the "holy place" and before the "most holy" place. It was small altar of one cubit length and one cubit breadth and two cubits height with four horns on its four corners. The altar was fully overlaid with gold. It was on this golden altar that Aaron burnt sweet incense every morning when he dressed the lamps, and when he lit lamps in the evening. It was the commandment of God that the incense should be burnt upon the lamps and offered at the golden altar as perpetual incense before the LORD throughout their generations (cf. Exodus 30:1-10).

Apostle John heard, in his vision, a voice from the four horns of the golden altar. The voice was of the sixth angel who said "Release the four angels who are bound at the great river Euphrates". The LORD prepared four angels to be released to kill the third of mankind at the specific hour, on the specific day, in the specific month and in the specific year. These four angels could be the same ones who held four winds at the four corners of the earth while another angel sealed 12,000 from each of the 12 tribes of Israel making up a specific number of 144,000, nothing more and nothing less.

River Euphrates has great significance in the scriptures. It was the land from wilderness and Lebanon up to great river Euphrates that the LORD promised to give to the children of Israel, after driving out Hittites from it. He promised to set the boundaries from the Red sea even unto the sea of the Philistines and from the desert unto the river Euphrates.

The LORD said to them to serve Him and none else that they may be blessed with their daily bread and water, and also to be free from sickness which He promised to take away from their midst. He promised to send the winged wasps, which are hornets, before them to drive out the Hivites, Canaanites, and the Hittites from before them. Is it not wonderful that God can drive out enemies of His children with hornets?

Yet, in doing so, the LORD said he will keep their enemies in the land for one year in order that the enemies may toil and keep the land fruitful for the children of Israel enjoy its fruit and to be free from laboring for their fruit. How wonderful was it that even as He kept their enemies in their land, for a short specified duration, the LORD's purpose was to do good for His children. It would seem that the enemies were in the land as if to harm them, and the enemies would feel that they had an edge over the children of Israel, but the LORD was intending to do good for His children. Later, the LORD said that He will drive them out slowly until the children of Israel are increased in number and competent to inherit the land.

Speaking about his enemies and idolaters Psalmist wrote:

"Truly you set them in slippery places; you make them fall to ruin" (Psalm 73:18 ESV)

"And we know that all things work together for good to them that love God, to them who are the called according to his purpose" (Romans 8:28)

However, the LORD expressly said to the children of Israel that they should neither make any covenant with those nations nor serve their gods; and doing so will be to a great snare for them. Much later, when King Solomon reigned over all kingdoms from the Euphrates River unto the land of the Philistines and unto the border of Egypt, all the kings over whom Solomon had authority brought to him gifts and served him all the days of his life.

Nevertheless, when Solomon went after the women from other nations and their gods, God rent his kingdom into two, and after his days the northern kingdom fell to idolatry. Hoshea was the nineteenth king in Israel and he is believed to have ruled the "House of Israel" during 732–721 BC.

None of the nineteen kings of the northern kingdom did what was pleasing to the LORD and their disobedience resulted in the northern kingdom, which was known as the "House of Israel" to be scattered all over the world. They have mixed up with many nations and, perhaps, this may be the reason why many of them including gentiles were disobedient to the LORD even in the end days (cf. Exodus 23:25-33; Deuteronomy 11:24; Joshua 1:4; 1 Kings 4:21; Revelation 9:20-21).

No wonder, John saw in his vision that the sixth angel poured out his bowl on the great river Euphrates, and it dried up to prepare the way for the kings from the east.

"The sixth angel poured out his bowl on the great river Euphrates, and its water was dried up, to prepare the way for the kings from the east" (Revelation 16:12)

John heard the number of the mounted troops which was twice ten thousand times ten thousand, and he saw the horses and the riders thereon. The power of the horses was in their mouths and in their tails, which were like serpents with heads by which they wounded mankind. They wore breastplates of the color of fire and of sapphire and of sulfur, and the heads of the horses were like lions' heads, and fire and smoke and sulfur came out of their mouths. By the fire and smoke and sulfur coming out of their mouths, which were three plagues, a third of mankind was killed.

In spite of the proclamation of Gospel during grace period, and in the last days before the return of Lord Jesus Christ, there was yet two-thirds of mankind, who did not repent of the works of their hands nor gave up "worshiping demons and idols of gold and silver and bronze and stone and wood, which cannot see or hear or walk, nor did they repent of their murders or their sorceries or their sexual immorality or their thefts" (cf. Revelation 9:20-21)

When Moses was 120 years old, and because he was not permitted by God to enter the Promised Land, he gave instructions to the children of Israel through Joshua and said he knew the rebellion of the children of Israel as to how stiff necked they were, and how much they would be in future after his death.

"For I know thy rebellion, and thy stiff neck: behold, while I am yet alive with you this day, ye have been rebellious against the LORD; and how much more after my death?" (Deuteronomy 31:27)

It is inexplicable as to why these generations from of old continuing into tribulation period did not believe in the Lord, even in spite of hearing the Gospel of Jesus Christ during grace period, and from 144,000 Jewish descendants. It is not known if they are chosen or not; or they were stubborn to refuse to yield to the truth of the Knowledge of the living God; and whatever may be the reason there will be people worshipping idols and incurring the wrath of God, even in the end of the days, until Jesus makes a physical appearance on this earth second time to establish His literal kingdom and to judge all the rebels.

The second "woe", of the three "woes" announced in Revelation Chapter 8:13, continues till the end of Revelation Chapter 11:14

CHAPTER 26
SECOND INTERLUDE

(From Revelation Chapter 10:1-11)

"And I saw another mighty angel come down from heaven, clothed with a cloud: and a rainbow was upon his head, and his face was as it were the sun, and his feet as pillars of fire" (Revelation 10:1)

This chapter deals with the little book that was open; the cry like that of a roaring lion of "another mighty angel", which resulted in seven thunders that uttered their voices; the voice from heaven forbidding John from writing details of the utterings that seven thunders produced; the cry that there should no more time for repentance be given; the voice ordering John to take the little book from "another mighty angel" and eat it up; the eating up of the book, which was sweet in taste but bitter in stomach.

Just as Revelation Chapter 7, which was not a continuation of the opening of the seals of the scroll, a group of five chapters viz. 10, 11, 12, 13 was not a continuation of the blowing of the trumpet. Chapter 6 contains the details of the opening of the six seals of the scroll and chapter 8 contains the details of opening of the seventh seal of the scroll. Thus the chapter 7 interposed between chapters 6 and 8 with the details of the sealing of 144,000 descendants from Israel, and the martyrs of "great tribulation" period.

There is similar interposition with a group of five chapters viz. 10 to 14 between chapters 9 and 15 as if to provide us an insight of what was to come in future, such as measuring the temple of God, the two witnesses, and protection of the children of Israel etc. Chapter 15 opens with seven angels having the seven last plagues; for in them is filled up the wrath of God. The seven angels start pouring their vials of judgment upon earth and earth dwellers in chapter 16.

When we consider the power "another mighty angel" wielded, his adornment and his authoritative movements, we cannot think that He was just an angel, but he was another angel, who was of exceptional strength, but of the same kind.

The word "another" used here is the translation of the Greek word Strong's# 243, which is "allos" which means "another of the same kind". If the word used was a translation of Greek word Strong's # 2087 "heterous", which means "another of a different kind", then there was possibility of interpreting that the angel referred to here was Lord Jesus.

This "another mighty angel" was clothed with cloud; he had a rainbow on his head; his face was as it were the sun, and his feet were as pillars of fire. Much of his description suits to assume that He was Jesus Christ, while the controversial view does not agree that he is Lord Jesus Christ.

The description of Lord Jesus Christ in Chapter 1 was, as the one who comes with clouds, and as the one who had on His head hairs which were like wool, as white as snow, and His eyes were as flaming fire. His feet were like fine brass, as if they burned in furnace and His voice as the sound of many waters; and every eye shall see Him, even those who pierced Him (for detailed text please read Revelation 1:7, 14-16)

Lord Jesus Christ was the only one who was found worthy to open the seven seals on the book, which had writing on both the sides. The writing on both the sides of the scroll (book) shows that it was legal document to possess the earth which he has purchased with His blood. Lord Jesus purchased us, not with silver or god, but with His precious blood shed on the cross of Calvary. Originally the earth was the Lord's when He created it; but when the LORD gave the earth to man he lost the earth to Satan when he transgressed the commandment of God and yielded to Satan. Now that Lord Jesus Christ purchased the earth and man He comes to take possession of them.

When "another mighty angel" came down from heaven, he had in his hand a little book open; and he set his right foot upon the sea and the left foot on the earth. This little book may not be the book which had seven seals on it that the Lamb was opening.

Apostle Paul wrote whole creation groans to be redeemed. We are sealed with the Holy Spirit of promise (Ephesians 1:13). We are not yet fully redeemed. The earth and the man will be fully redeemed when Lord Jesus Christ comes again.

"For we know that the whole creation has been groaning together in the pains of childbirth until now. And not only the creation, but we ourselves, who have the firstfruits of the Spirit, groan inwardly as we wait eagerly for adoption as sons, the redemption of our bodies. For in this hope we were saved. Now hope that is seen is not hope. For who hopes for what he sees? But if we hope for what we do not see, we wait for it with patience" (Romans 8:22-25 ESV)

The voice of the angel referred to in this chapter, was like that of roaring lion; and when he cried with loud voice, seven thunders uttered their voices. When John heard the voices from the seven thunders, he was about to write the details, but was forbidden to write by a voice, which he heard from heaven. The voice emphatically ordered him not to write the details but to seal them up.

The details as to what the seven thunders uttered are not recorded in the Bible, and it is not for us make conjectures as to what they uttered, or what the interpretation of those utterings could have been. There are some views about the voices that the seven thunders uttered, but it is not right to make conjectures. Any view expressed in violation of the command that Bible made is transgression of the command. Inasmuch as the Bible clearly forbade John from revealing them; no one is above the command; and any interpretation thereof, is private interpretation.

The "another mighty angel" stood upon the sea and upon the earth and lifted his hand to heaven and swore by the LORD, who lives forever and ever, who created heaven and everything therein, and the earth and everything therein, and the sea and everything therein, that the creation should not be given any more time to repent. His desire was that the mystery of God should be finished at the blowing of the seventh trumpet, as declared to the prophets.

John again heard, from heaven, the voice which said that he should go and take the little book from the hand of that "another might angel". John went to the said angel and said to him to give him the little book. The angel gave it to him saying "Take it, and eat it up; and it shall make thy belly bitter, but it shall be in thy mouth sweet as honey"

"And I went unto the angel, and said unto him, Give me the little book. And he said unto me, Take it, and eat it up; and it shall make thy belly bitter, but it shall be in thy mouth sweet as honey" (Revelation 10:9)

John took the little book out of the hand of the "another mighty angel" and ate it up. As the angel said, the book was sweet as honey in his mouth but as soon as he ate it his belly was bitter. The contents of the book were not seen, but when John ate it his belly was bitter, indicating that there would be great trials and persecutions.

Many times the word of God seems very pleasant in the beginning, as would promise prosperity on this earth, but as we search deep it shows us the truth, which is bitter.   The life on this earth is not a bed of roses for a believer, but full of trials and temptations, and yet the believer find solace in the Lord, who redeems the believer from all the troubles that he/she faces.

The "another mighty angel" said to John that he should prophesy again before many people, and nations, and tongues, and kings.

CHAPTER 27
FUTURE TEMPLE

(From Revelation Chapter 11:1-2)

"Then I was given a measuring rod like a staff, and I was told, "Rise and measure the temple of God and the altar and those who worship there, but do not measure the court outside the temple; leave that out, for it is given over to the nations, and they will trample the holy city for forty-two months" (Revelation 11:1-2 ESV)

The first two verses of Revelation Chapter 11 record a very interesting sign that would be seen in future before the second coming of Lord Jesus Christ.

John was given a reed like rod and the angel said to him to rise and measure the temple of God, and the altar and them that worship therein. The angel restricted him from measuring the outer court of the temple, and the holy city, which is Jerusalem, because they were given to the Gentiles to tread under foot for forty two months.

From these two verses it is inferred that there is going to be temple built, and there is going to be outer court to that temple, and Gentiles will tread not only the outer court of the temple but the whole city of Jerusalem as well, for a specified duration, which is forty two months. (Forty two months are equal to 3 ½ years, or 1260 days at the rate of 30 days in a month according to Hebrew calendar).

There are few references in the Bible that point to this future temple. Lord Jesus Christ mentioned about the "abomination of desolation" spoken of by Daniel the prophet. He said the abomination would stand in the holy place. The temple has "outer court", "holy place" and the "most holy" place whereas the whole city of Jerusalem is "holy city"

"So when you see the abomination of desolation spoken of by the prophet Daniel, standing in the holy place (let the reader understand)" (Matthew 24:15 ESV))

Daniel prophesied about the "abomination of desolation", and its related events (cf. Daniel 9:25-27; Daniel 11:31; and Daniel 12:11)

Apostle Paul referred to this temple wherein the "man of sin", who is also called "son of Perdition" otherwise known as "Antichrist" would sit and exalts himself as God (cf. 2 Thessalonians 2:3-9)

Lord Jesus Christ warned about Antichrist.

"Then if any man shall say unto you, Lo, here is Christ, or there; believe it not" (Matthew 24:23)

Apostle Paul warned not to allow anyone who would try to deceive believers saying Christ has already come. Some believers in Thessalonians had received a letter purportedly written by him saying Lord Jesus has already come. Therefore, the believers in Thessalonica were shaken in mind and were troubled about the destiny of their fathers who died already and their destiny after death.

Then, Paul wrote that that the said day will not come unless the rebellion comes first; and the man of lawlessness is revealed.

Among several interpretations one that stands out unique and convincing is that the Church will be "caught up" before the "great tribulation", and then the 70th week of Daniel's seventy-week-prophecy will commence.

"Let no one deceive you in any way. For that day will not come, unless the rebellion comes first, and the man of lawlessness is revealed, the son of destruction, who opposes and exalts himself against every so-called god or object of worship, so that he takes his seat in the temple of God, proclaiming himself to be God" (2 Thessalonians 2:3-4 ESV)

From the decree made by Artexerexes to rebuild Jerusalem, one week of seven years was determined, and after sixty two weeks of seven years each was the Messiah's crucifixion is prophesied. That is to say at the end of 69 weeks Messiah was to be cut off and it happened exactly as prophesied.

There is one more week of seven years that should come to pass; and it is delayed because the Church, which was a mystery in the Old Testament period, has come into existence at the end of sixty nine weeks of the said Daniel's prophecy. The last week of seven years commences after the church is "caught up" to be with the Lord forever and ever.

The "man of sin" will speak great things and blasphemies because power was given to him to continue for forty two months (3 ½ years), which is the "great tribulation" period. The children of Israel will be protected during this period for forty two months; and the "two witnesses" shall prophesy for a period of "a thousand two hundred and threescore days, clothed in sackcloth" (cf. Revelation 11:3; 12:14; 13:5)

Paul writes that apostasy would come first, and the "man of sin" who is "the son of Perdition" will be revealed only after the "restrainer" is "taken out of the way".

After the Herod's Temple was destroyed fully by Titus in AD 70, Jerusalem was fully plowed down and levelled to the ground in AD 135. There remained no trace even to guess where exactly Solomon's Temple stood. Currently there is "Dome of the Rock", under the control of Islam, on approximately at the site where Solomon's Temple and Herod's Temple stood.

Some researchers have also thought that the exact place, where the Herod's Temple stood, may be slightly north of the "dome of the rock" while some others say the exact site may be slightly south of the "dome of the rock". If any such view is true, then the "Dome of the Rock" would be in the area which is "given unto the Gentiles". In addition, according to scriptures, the holy city, which is Jerusalem, "shall they tread under foot forty and two months". In man's understanding these are very hard things to perceive; but God knows the future exactly, and we understand the future as revealed to us, with our finite knowledge.

The position of the future temple, if it is built, would be before the Ezekiel's Temple.

1. Tabernacle
2. Solomon's Temple
3. Zerubbabel/Herod's Temple
4. Future Temple
5. Ezekiel's Temple

- There was "Tabernacle", a portable structure, of the model of heavenly sanctuary, built according to the command and details given by God to Moses (cf. Exodus 25:9)

- A large Temple of the pattern of Tabernacle was built by King Solomon (cf. 1 Kings 6:2; This temple was destroyed by Nebuchadnezzar king of Babylon (2 Kings 25:1-7; Ezra 5:12)
- Zerubbabel, the governor, and Joshua, the son of Josedech, the high priest built a temple in place of Solomon Temple that was destroyed (cf. Ezra chapter 3:1-13; Haggai 1:1)
- Ezekiel prophesied about a temple that will be built during the thousand-year-reign of Lord Jesus Christ on this earth (cf. Ezekiel 41:1)

There are other views that the temple referred to in 2 Thessalonians 2 is believer's body, and the abomination that was spoken of was the Roman army standing in Jerusalem destroying the temple and the city in AD 70. However, that view leads to understand in the way preterists understand Daniel's seventy week prophecy, which gives no scope of proper explanation as to where the "great tribulation" would fit in Daniel's Prophecy.

If Preterists view is to be taken as the right interpretation of the seventy-week prophecy of Daniel, then it is already completed, and Jesus is already here in spiritual form. Their interpretation is, therefore, not a proper exegesis of the scripture.

According to the prophecy Antichrist will make a strong covenant with many for one week, and at the midpoint he will break the covenant; and will put an end to sacrifice and offering. The first half of 7 year-period, which is 3 ½ years, will be peaceful and the rest of the 3 ½ years will be the last days when the wrath of God is seen severely.

"And he shall make a strong covenant with many for one week, and for half of the week he shall put an end to sacrifice and offering. And on the wing of abominations shall come one who makes desolate, until the decreed end is poured out on the desolator." (Daniel 9:27 ESV)

CHAPTER 28
THE TWO WITNESSES PART I

(FROM REVELATION CHAPTER 11)

WHY TWO WITNESSES?

Lord Jesus said in the mouth of two or three witnesses every word may be established. This was based on the Mosaic Law as it is written in Deuteronomy 19:15. When Pharisees had an argument over His assertion that He is the light of the world and He who follows Him "shall not walk in darkness but shall have light of life" (cf. Matthew 18:16; John 8:12; John 8:17), Jesus said it is written in the Mosaic Law that the testimony of two men is true.

At the death of Jesus two men, who were Roman Government officials, viz. Nicodemus and rich man of Arimathaea, who that followed Jesus secretly, were witnesses to His death (cf. John 19:38, 39). The empty tomb of Jesus, after His resurrection, was witnessed by Simon Peter and John (John 20:1-8). The ascension of Lord Jesus Christ was witnessed by two men.

"It is also written in your law, that the testimony of two men is true" (John 8:17)

"And while they looked stedfastly toward heaven as he went up, behold, two men stood by them in white apparel" (Acts 1:10)

The pattern is followed in the Book of Revelation also that two witnesses come before Lord Jesus Christ steps on the Mount of

Olives. We, who are saved in the precious blood of Lord Jesus Christ, would have been caught up long before the two witnesses emerge on to the scene here on this earth. The two witnesses stand in testimony to the Lord Jesus Christ and His second advent on this earth.

The Antitypes mentioned are the culmination of the shadows and types mentioned in the Old Testament period. In the Old Testament Zechariah 4:3 the shadow of the two witnesses coming during 'great tribulation' period is recorded. The Menorah (the seven-candlesticks) is continually filled with oil coming from the two olive trees. This is imagery that the two witnesses are continually filled with the Holy Spirit during their ministry. Their ministry is not proclaiming the Gospel but it is of repentance.

During the period when the children of Israel were journeying in the wilderness they had the "Tabernacle", wherein in the Holy Place Aaron and priests lit up the seven lamps day and evening to make sure that the lamps never get extinguished. These seven lamp stands standing lit always is the Holy Place is "Menorah". God spoke to Moses and said to him to instruct Aaron that the seven lamps shall give light over the candle stick (cf. Numbers 8:2).

Much later after completion of their journey in the wilderness and with the passage of time, the children of Israel rejected "theocracy", which is the Government by direct rule by the LORD God, and then they rejected rule by Judges appointed by the LORD God. The LORD gave them a king according to their choice and he was Saul, who disobeyed God and his place was taken over by David, who was called by God as the "a man after mine own heart" (cf. Acts 13:22). After David's time was over

Solomon, his son by Bathsheba took over reins over the nation of Israel and built the "House of the LORD", which was called Solomon's temple.

As the history in the Bible and secular history proves Solomon's temple was destroyed; and after seventy years of captivity of the children of Israel in the land of Babylon, they returned to Jerusalem and built the temple, which was called Zerubbabel temple; after the name of Zerubbabel, the governor of the land, who helped Joshua the son of Josedech, who was the high priest; Nehemiah the son of Hachaliah, who in the palace at Shushan served King Ahasuerus; and Ezra the scribe.

In the Zerubbabel's temple there stood "a candlestick of gold, with a bowl upon the top of it and his seven lamps thereon, and seven pipes to the seven lamps". Instead of priests lighting up lights every day and every evening, a provision was made to supply oil from the two olive trees directly to the seven lamps through seven pipes.

The two olive trees stood one on the right hand side of the bowl, and the other on the left hand side of the bowl. Thus there was continuous flow of oil from the two olive trees to the seven lamps by pipes signifying continuous ministry by the Holy Spirit.

The oil represents Holy Spirit; the Two Olive trees represent the two witnesses. Holy Spirit continuously flowed from the Two Olive Trees to the Lamps in Zerubbabel's Temple, and thus will be the ministry of Holy Spirit flowing continuously through the two witnesses as long as they do their ministry of repentance in the end days. (cf. Zechariah 4:2-14)

"Then I said to him, "What are these two olive trees on the right and the left of the lampstand?" And a second time I answered and said to him, "What are these two branches of the olive trees, which are beside the two golden pipes from which the golden oil is poured out?" He said to me, "Do you not know what these are?" I said, "No, my lord." Then he said, "These are the two anointed ones who stand by the Lord of the whole earth."" (Zechariah 4:11-14 ESV)

CHAPTER 29
THE TWO WITNESSES PART II

(FROM REVELATION CHAPTER 11)

WHO ARE THESE TWO WITNESSES?

Although Bible does not name who the two witnesses are, yet from the description in Malachi and other references it could be inferred that they are probably Moses and Elijah. Prophecy in Zechariah 4:2-14 gives us the primary purpose of the two witnesses. They stand as undeniable witnesses to the LORD and their ministry is the ministry of repentance.

The different views are: they are:

1. Moses and Elijah;
2. Moses and Enoch/Elijah and Enoch;
3. Moses and John/ Elijah and John
4. None of them but two unnamed individuals
5. Not human beings but they are symbolical.

MOSES AND ELIJAH

From the Old Testament scriptures it is seen that there are two men who were only half way through their ministry and they were Moses and Elijah.

Moses grew up in Pharaoh's residence and after forty years, kills an Egyptian to save a Hebrew and then flees home; for the next forty years he was in Midian, and during the next forty years he was chosen by God as leader of the children of Israel to lead them to the Promised Land. With God's help he redeems physically the children of Israel and leads them through the wilderness for forty years.

(2) MOSES AND ELIJAH/ELIJAH AND ENOCH

Second possibility is about Enoch because he was taken alive into heaven. Enoch was not a Jew. Some depend upon Paul's writing that it is appointed unto everyone to die once (cf. Hebrew 9:27); but that verse does not apply here, because there others, who were brought to life by Jesus viz. Lazarus, the daughter of Jairus, dead man at city called Nain etc. had their natural death again.

(3) MOSES AND JOHN/ELIJAH AND JOHN

Third Possibility is John with either Moses or Elijah. The opinion is based on the last verse of chapter 10; but that is not correct interpretation of the scriptures as John continued to be the writer of the book of Revelation and died of very old age.

(4) NONE OF THEM BUT TWO UN-NAMED INDIVIAUALS

Fourth possibility is that God may give powers to any two men of His choice in the last days to His two witnesses; this could be but more reliable is the view that the two witnesses are Moses and Elijah.

(5) NOT HUMAN BEINGS BUT THEY ARE SYMBOLICAL

Fifth possibility is that the two witnesses are not men at all; but symbolic representation; this is not right because the two witnesses did miracles.

In Zechariah Chapter 4 there is shadow of these two witnesses is shown. In the Zerubbabel Temple Joshua, the son of Josedech, the high priest served as priest, and Zerubbabel was the governor of that land. The menorah with seven candlesticks was continually fed with oil to burn in the "holy place". The oil refers to Holy Spirit and this will be fulfilled in the last seven year period of Daniel's prophesied seventy weeks.

By ruling out all other possibilities it can be safely concluded that that the two witnesses who would come during the Great Tribulation period are Moses and Elijah. They will continually be filled with Holy Spirit and bear the testimony of Jesus Christ and their ministry is the ministry of repentance.

Nonetheless, after their ministry is completed God gives power to the beast that comes from the bottomless pit to kill them. People rejoice over their death; but then God raises them after three and half days and will be caused by the LORD to ascend into heaven (cf. Revelation 11:7-12)

CHAPTER 30
THAT ROCK WAS CHRIST

MOSES SMITES THE ROCK

"And did all drink the same spiritual drink: for they drank of that spiritual Rock that followed them: and that Rock was Christ. But with many of them God was not well pleased: for they were overthrown in the wilderness. Now these things were our examples, to the intent we should not lust after evil things, as they also lusted" (1 Corinthians 10:4-6)

Writing to Corinthians Apostle Paul says to them that they should not be ignorant that the children of Israel, during the period of Moses, passed under the cloud, and passed through the Red sea, which signified that they were baptized unto Moses in the cloud and in the sea. They all ate the same spiritual food and drank of that spiritual Rock that followed them; and that rock was Christ.

It was when the children of Israel were redeemed from the bondage of slavery under Pharaoh in Egypt that they had their physical deliverance. Except for their doubting nature, and rebellion, they could have entered the Promised Land very quickly after coming out of Egypt; but because they murmured against the LORD again and again, they had to wander in the wilderness for forty years.

The children of Israel left wilderness of "Sin" and came to Rephidim, where there was no water for them to drink. They, who were slaves under Pharaoh for four hundred years, murmured against God. They chided with Moses and demanded water to drink. When Moses asked them as to why they were tempting the LORD, they in their thirst, retorted asking if he brought them from out of Egypt to kill them, their children and their cattle with thirst.

Moses was deeply distressed and cried to the Lord to help him know as to what he should do to the children of Israel, who were ready to stone him. The LORD answered and said to him to take with him the elders of Israel and his rod that he used to smite the river in order to turn the waters into blood, and go to the rock in Horeb. The LORD said to Moses to smite the said rock upon which He will stand and water will come out of it that the people may drink. Moses obeyed the LORD in the sight of the elders of Israel. Thus the children of Israel drank water from the rock. Moses called the place "Massah" (which means temptation), and "Meribah" (which means chiding or strife), because the children of Israel tempted the LORD and doubted if He was there among them or not (cf. Exodus 17:1-7)

A similar situation occurred when the children of Israel dwelt in Kadesh in the desert of "Zin", where there was no water. They gathered together and strove with Moses and Aaron and questioned if God wanted that they die in the wilderness just as their fathers died in Egypt when they were slaves. They also questioned Moses and Aaron as to why they brought them out of the land of Egypt if their desire was not to see that their cattle die? They called the place as "evil place" and said the place had neither seed, nor figs, or vines, or pomegranates, or water to drink.

The glory of the LORD appeared to them there and the LORD spoke to Moses when Moses and Aaron went out unto the door of the Tabernacle of the congregation and fell prostrate before the LORD. The LORD said to him to take his rod, which he used for turning the river water into blood, and gather the children of Israel and Aaron, and speak to the rock before their eyes. The LORD said that the rock will give forth his water, and that Moses shall bring forth the water out of the rock and give them and their cattle to drink.

As commanded by God Moses took the rod from before the LORD. He and Aaron gathered the children of Israel before the rock and Moses spoke angrily to them and called them 'rebels'. In his anger he asked them if they should bring forth water from the rock and lifted up his hand and smote it with his rod twice.

No doubt, water came forth abundantly and the congregation and their cattle drank from the rock; but the act of Moses was highly displeasing to the LORD. The LORD knew the needs of His people and provided water to them and their cattle; but the anger of Moses towards the children of Israel seemed to be greater than the displeasure of the LORD towards the children of Israel. God counted the violation by Moses of His command as very serious disobedience.

There was reason why the LORD said to Moses to speak to the rock rather than strike it. First time, when they were at Rephidim the LORD said Moses to smite the rock and it gave water but second time when they were at Kadesh in the desert of Zin the LORD said to Moses to speak to the rock and it will give forth his water; but alas! Moses smote it. That Rock was Christ and He was to be smitten only once, in future, while in his incarnation as Savior. When Moses smote the Rock the Lord, the intended purpose was not shown to the people of Israel and he did not sanctify the LORD in the midst of the children of Israel.

"Because ye trespassed against me among the children of Israel at the waters of Meribah-Kadesh, in the wilderness of Zin; because ye sanctified me not in the midst of the children of Israel" (Deuteronomy 32:51)

Later, speaking to Joshua, Moses recollected his error. He said the LORD did not accept his repentance because his disobedience was great and it projected a wrong meaning to the offer that the LORD made. The LORD said to him that he shall not go over Jordan and he should go the top of Pisgah, and lift his eyes in all the four directions and see the land with his eyes. (cf. Numbers 20:8-10; Deuteronomy 3:21-29; 1 Corinthians 10:4, 6)

However, Moses appeared to Peter, James and his brother John at the transfiguration of Lord Jesus and it shows that Moses is in heaven. We have, therefore, enough reason to believe that he will come as one of the two witnesses and bear testimony for the Lord thus completing his unfinished assignment.

CHAPTER 31
ELIJAH CALLS FIRE FROM HEAVEN

"Then Moab rebelled against Israel after the death of Ahab. And Ahaziah fell down through a lattice in his upper chamber that was in Samaria, and was sick: and he sent messengers, and said unto them, Go, enquire of Baalzebub the god of Ekron whether I shall recover of this disease" (2 Kings 1:1-2)

After the death of King Ahab his son Ahazia took over reigns of Northern Kingdom of Israel which was at its lowest ebb in their spiritual life. Idolatry started during the period of Jeroboam the first king of Northern Kingdom and during the period of Ahab his wicked wife Jezebel introduced "Baal" worship. The children of Israel have become so addicted to worshipping "Baal" that when Elijah pleaded them to return to God and accept Him as LORD, they did not speak a word. Subsequently he challenged them and proved that the God Abraham, of Isaac and of Israel was the true God.

Now when Ahazia became King he did evil in the sight of the LORD just as his father did. One day he fell through lattice in his upper chamber in Samaria and lay sick. In order to know whether he would be healed or not he sent his messengers with instructions to go and inquire "Baal-zeebub" the god of "Ekron". Ekron was an ancient city of Philistines. Joshua did not subdue it but it was allotted to him in the division of the land initially to Judah and later on to Dan (cf. Joshua 13:3; Joshua 15:11, 45-46; 19:43. The name of the city Ekron figures in the narration when Philistines feared presence of the Ark of the Covenant in their land and the proposed to send it back to Israel (Cf. 1Sa 5:10; 6:16-17)

Hebrew Word Strong's# 1176 "Ba`al Z@buwb" is transliterated as "bah'-al zeb-oob'", originated from Strong's# 1168 and 2070 and its definition is "Baal of (the) Fly; Baal-Zebub, a special deity of the Ekronites:--"Baal-zebub" and is also called the "Baal of the Flies" or "lord of the flies".

Lord Jesus Christ referred to "Baal-zebub" mentioned in the Old Testament as "Beelzebul", which in Greek was called "Beelzebul" (Greek Strong's# 954 transliterated as "beh-el-zeb-ool'" of Chaldee origin (by parody on H1176) which "dung-god"; Beelzebul, a name of Satan, Beelzebub.

"But when the Pharisees heard it, they said, This fellow doth not cast out devils, but by Beelzebub the prince of the devils. And Jesus knew their thoughts, and said unto them, Every kingdom divided against itself is brought to desolation; and every city or house divided against itself shall not stand: And if Satan cast out Satan, he is divided against himself; how shall then his kingdom stand? And if I by Beelzebub cast out devils, by whom do your children cast them out? therefore they shall be your judges. But if I cast out devils by the Spirit of God, then the kingdom of God is come unto you" (Matthew 12:24-28)

The LORD was highly displeased with Ahazia who sent messengers to Ekron to inquire from the Baal-zebub "Lord of the Flies", whom he was worshipping to know if he would be healed or not. The LORD therefore, sent Elijah the Tishbite to question him if there was no God in Israel that Ahazia should send messengers to inquire from someone who is lord over flies.

It is so pathetic that man worships creation rather than Creator. Flies are indeed created marvelously by God but they are creation and not creator. They are worth only to be seen as creation and do not deserve any worship. Satan has closed the understanding of people who condescend to worshipping flies, snakes, trees, and rocks. Bible condemns worshiping creation rather than creator.

Messengers of Ahazia returned to the king and the king asked him as to why they returned. They said to him that they saw a man who ordered them to return to say to the king that to question him if there was no God in Israel that he should send them to inquire from Baal-zebub, the god of Ekron if he would be healed or not. The Messengers also said that the man said to them that the king will be bed-ridden until his death. Ahazia was curious to know who that man was, and how he looked like. They answered and said to him that he "wore a garment of hair, with a belt of leather about his waist." Ahazia recognized him and said, "It is Elijah the Tishbite."

Ahazia, in his authority as King, sent a captain over fifty men with his fifty men to bring Elijah to him. The captain went up to Elijah who was sitting on the top of a hill and said to him "O man of God, the king says, 'Come down.'" The captain in his authority and power, vested in him by the king, was ordering Elijah the Tishbite who was sent by the Almighty God the King of kings. It was derogatory to order the "man of God" to come down from the place where he was sitting and stand before the king of earthly kingdom. Elijah answered the captain of fifty saying "If I am a man of God, let fire come down from heaven and consume you and your fifty." Elijah called fire from heaven and the fire came down from heaven and consumed the captain and his fifty men.

When a similar situation occurred in the New Testament period, when Lord Jesus Christ was not received by Samaritans, his disciples James and John inquired of Lord Jesus Christ if they should call for fire from heaven and consume them just as Elijah did; but Lord Jesus prevented such drastic action. He was so compassionate towards those who did not receive Him and rebuked His disciples.

"But he turned, and rebuked them, and said, Ye know not what manner of spirit ye are of. For the Son of man is not come to destroy men's lives, but to save them. And they went to another village" (cf. Luke 9:51-56)

Lord Jesus came into this world in the form of a servant and in the likeness of man and died on the cross taking our sin upon Him even though He was sinless. He was buried and was raised by God. Paul writes that whoever confesses Jesus as Lord and believes in heart that God raised Him from the dead will be saved. Lord Jesus promised that whoever believes in Him shall not perish but have everlasting life. (cf. Romans 10:9 and John 3:16)

Ahazia sent to Elijah another captain of fifty men with his fifty men to bring him, and the captain added his power to the king's power, and said to the man of God, "O man of God, this is the king's order, 'Come down quickly!'" but Elijah answered saying "'If I am a man of God, let fire come down from heaven and consume you and your fifty' Then the fire of God came down from heaven and consumed him and his fifty".

As if this was not enough for Ahazia he sent a third captain of fifty men with his fifty men to bring Elijah to his presence. This time the third captain fell on his knees and begged Elijah saying, "O man of God, please let my life, and the life of these fifty servants of yours, be precious in your sight. Behold, fire came down from heaven and consumed the two former captains of fifty men with their fifties, but now let my life be precious in your sight."

Before Elijah called fire from heaven this time the angel of the LORD said to him to go with the third captain fearlessly and, therefore, he went with him and said to the king "Thus says the LORD, 'Because you have sent messengers to inquire of Baal-zebub, the god of Ekron—is it because there is no God in Israel to inquire of his word?—therefore you shall not come down from the bed to which you have gone up, but you shall surely die.'"

According to the word of the LORD by the mouth of Elijah, Ahazia the king died. (cf. 2 Kings 1-18)

CHAPTER 32
WAS JOHN THE BAPTIST ELIJAH?

Angel Gabriel appeared to Zachariah the priest, when he went into the temple to offer incense, according to his turn. Zechariah and Elizabeth were stricken in old age, and Elizabeth was barren all her life. The angel said to Zechariah that his wife Elizabeth will bear a son, who should be named as "John" and John will go before Lord Jesus, in the spirit and power of Elijah, "to turn the hearts of the fathers to the children, and the disobedient to the wisdom of the just; to make ready a people prepared for the Lord". (cf. Luke 1:13-17)

Moses wrote in Deuteronomy 18:15-18 that the LORD will raise, unto the children of Israel, a Prophet like him, whom they should hearken.

Lord Jesus questioned multitudes if they thought that John the Baptist was as weak as a reed, which can easily be shaken by the wind, or a man clothed in soft raiment. He said that those who wear soft raiment are in kings' house. He went on saying that it was written about John the Baptist that the LORD will send a messenger heralding His imminent arrival. He was sent to prepare way and to remove obstruction from the path of the Lord that they may accept Him as their Messiah. Isaiah and Malachi prophesied about John and Lord Jesus (cf. Malachi 3:1; Isaiah 40:3; Matthew 11:7-11; Luke 1:76).

"The voice of him that crieth in the wilderness, Prepare ye the way of the LORD, make straight in the desert a highway for our God" (Isaiah 40:3)

John lived an ascetic life similar to that of Elijah and had a leather girdle around his loins and raiment of camel's hair, and ate locusts and honey. He preached "kingdom of heaven" and sought people to repent (cf. Matthew 3:1-5; 2 Kings 1:8).

The Jews sent priests and Levites from Jerusalem to "Betherbara" beyond Jordan where John was baptizing and they inquired his credentials. John said He was not the Christ, and when they asked him if he was Elijah, he said he was not Elijah, and when they asked him if he was prophet, he said he was not a prophet.

John's mission was to bear witness of Jesus Christ, who was coming after him, yet He was before him. Lord Jesus Christ was superior to John, and was to be honored more than John. Law was given by Moses, but grace and truth came by Lord Jesus Christ, of whom the word of God says:

"In the beginning was the Word, and the Word was with God, and the Word was God". (John 1:1)

"And the Word was made flesh, and dwelt among us, (and we beheld his glory, the glory as of the only begotten of the Father,) full of grace and truth" (John 1:14)

John said he was not worthy to unloosen the latchet of the shoe of Lord Jesus Christ, who was coming after him and later, pointing to Lord Jesus, he said He was the Lamb of God, who takes away the sin of the world (cf. John 1:19-28).

John the Baptist said to Herod that it was unlawful to marry wife of Philip, who was Herod's brother and for saying the truth, he became victim of the wrath of Herod, who killed him, for the sake of Herodias. Thus the ministry of John the Baptist ended.

When Herod heard that Jesus was doing miracles he was perplexed. He heard some say that John the Baptist arose from the dead, and some said Elijah had appeared, and some said one of the prophets of old rose from the dead. Therefore, he sought to see Jesus. (cf. Luke 9:7-9)

At the transfiguration of Lord Jesus on the high mount (which was perhaps Mount Tabor), Moses and Elijah appeared to Peter, James and John his brother. They all saw the face of Jesus shining as sun, and his raiment was white as the light. As they came down the mount they asked Jesus as to why the scribes were saying that Elijah must first come. "Jesus answered and said to them that "Elijah does come, and he will restore all things. But I tell you that Elijah has already come, and they did not recognize him, but did to him whatever they pleased. So also the Son of Man will certainly suffer at their hands." Then the disciples understood that he was speaking to them of John the Baptist" (cf. Matthew 17:10-13)

John the Baptist denied that he was Elijah or Messiah. Malachi prophesied that a messenger would come as forerunner before the Lord, and as prophesied John the Baptist came, in the spirit and power of Elijah, as the forerunner of Lord Jesus at his first advent and Elijah will come as the forerunner of Lord Jesus Christ at His second advent.

There are two distinct prophecies, often confused, in Malachi. Malachi 3:1 deals with the first advent of Lord Jesus Christ, and Malachi 4: 5-6 deals with His second coming. Forerunner for the first advent of Lord Jesus Christ was John the Baptist, and because they did not accept John the Baptist, who was in spirit and power of Elijah, as the forerunner of Jesus, they denied

Jesus as their Messiah. Elijah will surely come, as one of the two witnesses, before the second advent of Lord Jesus Christ.

"Behold, I will send my messenger, and he shall prepare the way before me: and the Lord, whom ye seek, shall suddenly come to his temple, even the messenger of the covenant, whom ye delight in: behold, he shall come, saith the LORD of hosts" (Malachi 3:1)

"Behold, I will send you Elijah the prophet before the coming of the great and dreadful day of the LORD: And he shall turn the heart of the fathers to the children, and the heart of the children to their fathers, lest I come and smite the earth with a curse" (Malachi 4:5-6)

"For all the prophets and the law prophesied until John. And if ye will receive it, this is Elias, which was for to come. He that hath ears to hear, let him hear" (Matthew 11:13-15)

John was physically not Elijah, but he came in the spirit and power of Elijah. Jews were expecting that Elijah will come physically before Messiah does. Jesus said to them that Elijah has already come in the form of John, who was in spirit and power of Elijah, which was contrary to their expectation,. That is the reason why Jews did not believe Jesus as their Messiah.

CHAPTER 33
THE TWO WITNESSES PART III

(FROM REVELATION CHAPTER 11)

THE MINISTRY OF TWO WITNESSES

"And I will grant authority to my two witnesses, and they will prophesy for 1,260 days, clothed in sackcloth." (Revelation 11:3 ESV)

The LORD grants the two witnesses His authority to prophecy in sackcloth for 1260 days which shows that their ministry is not for proclaiming the Gospel but to repent on behalf of His people. Accordingly they do witness for the LORD in sackcloth on behalf of His people.

There are instances in the Old Testament period when the LORD commanded His prophets to repent on behalf of His people.

Micah the prophet said he will lament and wail. Stripping naked could mean to fully remove clothing from the body and repent, or it could also mean putting away the garment and the shoe, which in itself is an indication of humility. Tautology of the word 'naked' in all the cases would give a wrong meaning. An example or two are mentioned here to show that the word "naked" cannot be taken as literal:

1. "at that time the LORD spoke by Isaiah the son of Amoz, saying, "Go, and loose the sackcloth from your waist and take off your sandals from your feet," and he did so, walking naked and barefoot"

(Isaiah 20:2 ESV) Here, the phrase "naked and barefoot" is a sign of mourning.

2. "But David went up the ascent of the Mount of Olives, weeping as he went, barefoot and with his head covered. And all the people who were with him covered their heads, and they went up, weeping as they went" (2 Samuel 15:30 ESV)

3. "Therefore I said: "Look away from me;   let me weep bitter tears; do not labor to comfort me concerning the destruction of the daughter of my people." (Isaiah 22:4 ESV)

4. "For this I will lament and wail; I will go stripped and naked; I will make lamentation like the jackals, and mourning like the ostriches" Micah 1:8

5. Pass on your way, inhabitants of Shaphir, in nakedness and shame; the inhabitants of Zaanan do not come out; the lamentation of Beth-ezel shall take away from you its standing place. (Micah 1:11)

6. "And he too stripped off his clothes, and he too prophesied before Samuel and lay naked all that day and all that night. Thus it is said, "Is Saul also among the prophets?"" 1 Samuel 19:24

In all these cases Isaiah, David, Micah and Saul repented either in 'sackcloth' or 'naked and barefoot', or 'stripped and naked' or in 'nakedness and shame'. It could mean, in all good sense that they had put off their outer garments and shoe, inasmuch as they stood as mediators on behalf of people before the LORD, just as priests in the Tabernacle did between people and God.

However, in the case of Isaiah 22:4 the phrase would mean that the defeated prisoners would be humiliated by the conquerors and they are stripped naked. It was to show how the king of

Assyria deals with the Egyptian prisoners, and the Ethiopian captives, irrespective of their age, naked and barefoot, even with their buttocks uncovered, to the shame of Egypt.

God was teaching lessons to the children of Israel by His word through Isaiah the son of Amoz, saying "Go and loose the sackcloth from off thy loins, and put off thy shoe from thy foot". Isaiah did as the LORD commanded him to do.

It is interesting to note here that after the Church is "caught up" to meet the Lord in the air, the remnant on the earth is no longer under the grace period such as those during the Church period were. We, the believers in this age are, therefore, greatly blessed people. We were once sinners and yet by confessing our sins to God through the only mediator Lord Jesus Christ, are saved by grace through faith. The remnant is governed by the commandments and conventions of Old Testament period.

The miracles the two witnesses perform are similar to the ones performed my Moses and Elijah by the power of God. Moses turned water into blood at the command of God and Elijah brought fire from heaven according to the will of God. Elijah could shut the heaven for three and half years, by the power of God that it may not rain, and when it rained when he prayed after three and half years.

These two witnesses, who are the representatives of the power of God on earth, stand before the LORD of the earth as the two olive trees and the two lampstands. They are under the protection of the LORD until their ministry is fulfilled. The LORD limited their service to Him to three and half years.

If anyone hurts them fire pours from their mouths and it consumes their enemies. The pouring out of fire from their mouths could be similar to the fire that Elijah brought from heaven or it could be literal fire from their mouths.

Their enemies are doomed and killed by fire if they attempt to hurt them. They have the power for 1260 days to shut the sky from raining and to turn the water into blood and also to strike the earth with every kind of plague as often as they desire.

According as God decided the duration of the testimony the two witnesses cannot be beyond forty two months. The ministry of these two witnesses lasts exactly for three and half years and the beast that comes from abyss, not before they complete their testimony for the Lord, conquers and kills them. They will be conquered and killed by the beast that comes out of the bottomless pit. The beast can neither come out of the abyss nor could do any harm to them unless the power was given to it by the LORD. The people rejoice over their death; but they are brought to life by God after three and half days.

The earth-dwellers consisting of all the people and their generations of different languages and nations will see the dead bodies of the two witnesses and rejoice so much over them that they make merry by sending gifts one to another.

The limited ministry of the two witnesses also gives us a clear understanding that everyone's ministry for the Lord is limited by God according to His will and pleasure. After the ministry of any individual or group of believers is accomplished according to the purpose of the LORD he/they will be removed from the earth. Stephen's short duration of ministry and his stand for the Lord stand as unique example and justify such an appellation.

The Lord died in Jerusalem, which has become spiritually like sinful cities of old, viz. "Sodom and Egypt"; in its street will lie the dead bodies of the two witnesses for three and half days. The city is symbolically called Sodom and Egypt.

The mention of Sodom and Egypt is to denote the wickedness of Sodom and the slavery in Egypt respectively. The city where the dead bodies of the two witnesses lie for three and half day is compared to the wickedness of Sodom, very much known for sodomy, mentioned in Genesis Chapters 18 and 19. This city is also compared to Egypt where the children of Israel suffered persecution, and slavery under the bondage of Pharaoh.

The Spirit of life from God enters the two witnesses at the end of three and half days and they stand up on their feet. When people see that they have regained their lives they will be sore afraid. A great voice is heard from heaven saying to them "Come up hither". Their enemies see their ascension up to heaven in a cloud. A great earthquake occurs at that time and a tenth part of the city falls. In the earthquake seen were seven thousand slain men. The remnant were seen frightened and gave glory to the God of heaven. With this second woe is past and next comes the third one quickly. (cf. Rev.11: 7-14)

CHAPTER 34
THE WOMAN, THE MAN CHILD AND
THE DRAGON PART I

(FROM REVELATION CHAPTER 12)

INTRODUCTION

If Satan had known that crucifixion of Jesus would bring redemption for mankind he would have done as much double the work as to make sure that Jesus escaped the death on the cross; but Satan was taken by surprise. It pleased the Father to bruise the Son on the cross on behalf of us in order that we may receive salvation free of cost.

Satan thought by handing over Jesus to die on the cross he would crush Jesus on the cross, but Lord Jesus Christ, who is the "seed of the woman" fulfilled the scriptures by crushing his head on the cross. There is more surprise waiting for Satan to see how his final defeat will be at the hands of Lord Jesus Christ in the end days. Does not Satan know scriptures? Well, he knows the scriptures but he cannot perceive them and do his followers.

"The natural person does not accept the things of the Spirit of God, for they are folly to him, and he is not able to understand them because they are spiritually discerned" (1 Corinthians 2:14 ESV)

John 3:16b says "...that whoever believes in him should not perish but have eternal life".

The burial, resurrection and ascension of Jesus Christ gave us hope that we will remain dead but rise and ascend to meet the Lord in the air and be with Him forever and ever.

The secret things belong to God and they are concealed to be unraveled in the last days. Daniel was asked to seal up the book of Prophesy.

"But thou, O Daniel, shut up the words, and seal the book, even to the time of the end: many shall run to and fro, and knowledge shall be increased" (Daniel 12:4)

However, God has revealed the end time events in the book of Revelation the only book which says:

"Blessed is the one who reads aloud the words of this prophecy, and blessed are those who hear, and who keep what is written in it, for the time is near" (Revelation 1:3 ESV)

It is only those who have Holy Spirit indwelling them will understand the mysteries recorded in the Bible to the extent God allows them to understand. "He who has an ear, let him hear what the Spirit says to the churches." Revelation 3:22

Bible comes very seriously upon those who do not attempt to find out what is written in the word of God. Scripture supports scripture, and therefore, every effort should be made to understand by referring to prophecies and other references. God speaks to each individual in His own way.

CHAPTER 35
THE WOMAN

(FROM REVELATION CHAPTER 12)

Revelation Chapter 12 is one of the important chapters in the Bible that deals with a crucial theme. It is, therefore, imperative that endeavors should be made to understand who the woman, man-child, and the dragon, mentioned in this chapter are.

This chapter contains past, present and future history of man, Satan, Israel, the fall of man, and redemption of man as also of the earth by the blood of Lord Jesus Christ.

"And there appeared a great wonder in heaven; a woman clothed with the sun, and the moon under her feet, and upon her head a crown of twelve stars: And she being with child cried, travailing in birth, and pained to be delivered" (Revelation 12:1-2)

The woman is described to have been clothed with sun; she has moon under her feet and she has on her head a crown of twelve stars.

From the scriptures it is evident that God established His covenant through Abraham, Isaac, and Jacob. Israel is chosen nation by God and He called them as His people. The blessings, covenants and promises belonged to them. Although He chastened them several times His love for them is undying and He is not yet through with them.

The symbolism of sun, moon and twelve stars comes from Genesis 37:9-10 where Joseph dreamt a dream in which he saw sun, moon and eleven stars bowing to him.

"Then he dreamed another dream and told it to his brothers and said, "Behold, I have dreamed another dream. Behold, the sun, the moon, and eleven stars were bowing down to me." But when he told it to his father and to his brothers, his father rebuked him and said to him, "What is this dream that you have dreamed? Shall I and your mother and your brothers indeed come to bow ourselves to the ground before you?" (Genesis 37:9-10 ESV)

The woman who is clothed in sun represents Jacob, an emblem of truth, majesty and glory; and the moon, representation of Rachel, under her feet as though she walked on her, and the twelve stars (Joseph and his eleven brothers), who represent the twelve tribes of Israel.

The woman was pregnant crying out in labor pains to give birth to the child, who is to rule with a rod of iron. She escaped all the harm the dragon intended to bring upon her and she gave birth to the child. A great gap is seen between verses 5 and 6. Verse 5 speaks of the birth of Jesus, who will rule in future with a rod of iron. After accomplishing His mission on the earth He ascended into heaven and seated on the right hand of the Majesty. Verse 6 speaks of woman fleeing into the wilderness, where she has a place prepared of God that she should be fed for 1260 days.

The Lord came into this world as a "Lamb of God" who takes away the sin of the world. He accomplished His purpose and ascended into heaven and seated on the right hand of the Majesty. He comes back as a "Lion of the tribe of Judah" to rule with a rod of iron (cf. Rev. 5:5; Psalm 2:9)

Virgin Mary the earthly mother of Jesus, her espoused bridegroom Joseph, and the child Jesus fled to Egypt and lived there for nearly ten years, until the death of Herod, which is surely more than 1260 days. They escaped to Egypt in compliance to the instructions they received from an angel of the LORD. The instructions were that they should escape from Herod, who was attempting to kill infant Jesus.

After ascension of Lord Jesus Christ, the dragon went after the woman to persecute her; however the woman fled into wilderness and God protected her and nourished her for 1260 days. Such a thing as Mary fleeing into the wilderness, or Church fleeing into the wilderness are not found in the Bible.

CHAPTER 36
THE DRAGON

(FROM REVELATION CHAPTER 12)

In the meanwhile there appeared another sign in heaven. There was seen a great red dragon that had seven heads and ten horns and seven crowns upon his heads, which is in indication that the dragon wielded great power. Believer in Christ should realize that Satan is very powerful, but he cannot do any harm to the child of God until he is in the Lord. A child of God should be careful to take refuge in the Lord, because it is not possible for man to defeat Satan without taking the help of Lord Jesus Christ.

Apostle Paul warned in Ephesians 6:10-18 that our battle is not against flesh and blood "but against principalities, against powers, against the rulers of the darkness of this world, against spiritual wickedness in high places"

The dragon is also called the Serpent, or Satan, or the devil, or adversary, who with his tail drew the third part of the stars of heaven and cast them to the earth. In spite of Satan falling from heaven he has access to heaven. He continues to have access to heaven and accuse the brethren constantly until Michael the archangel and his angels wage a war against him and the dragon and his angels are defeated.

It is evident from Job 1:6 that Satan came into the presence of God "from going to and fro in the earth, and from walking up and down in it". Then, Job 1:7 and 8 show that God challenged Satan to test Job and not vice versa.

"Now there was a day when the sons of God came to present themselves before the LORD, and Satan came also among them" (Job 1:6)

"And the LORD said to Satan, 'Have you considered my servant Job, that there is none like him on the earth, a blameless and upright man, who fears God and turns away from evil?'" (Job 1:8 ESV)

When the dragon came down to earth he also brought with him a third part of the stars of heaven and cast of them on the earth. The third part of the stars is the angels, who stood by the dragon in his pride, are angels who are fallen.

The dragon stood before the woman who was ready to give birth to the child. The aim of the dragon was to devour the child as soon as He was born. The child was none other than Jesus, who was identified here as the one who rules with a rod of iron. Jesus escaped all attempts of Satan to defeat Him; rather He defeated Satan at the cross and ascended into heaven after accomplishing His purpose.

The dragon pursues the woman and sends out a flood of water to be swept away by the flood, but the earth helps the woman by opening its mouth and swallowing the flood of water.

CHAPTER 37
THE MAN-CHILD

(FROM REVELATION CHAPTER 12)

The man-child born to the woman was Lord Jesus Christ, who was Jewish Messiah. There are prophesies about Him in the Old Testament. Isaiah 9:6 is a prophecy of about Him who was to be born, and Isaiah 53 contains prophesy about the Lord's death on behalf of us; and Psalm 16: 10 is a prophecy about Lord's resurrection. Jesus Himself spoke in Luke 18:33 and Matthew 10:33 about His resurrection. The prophecy about His rule with a rod of iron is in Psalm 2:9

"For unto us a child is born, unto us a son is given: and the government shall be upon his shoulder: and his name shall be called Wonderful, Counsellor, The mighty God, The everlasting Father, The Prince of Peace" (Isaiah 9:6)

"Surely he hath borne our griefs, and carried our sorrows: yet we did esteem him stricken, smitten of God, and afflicted" (Isaiah 53:4)

"For thou wilt not leave my soul in hell; neither wilt thou suffer thine Holy One to see corruption" (Psalms 16:10)

"I will tell of the decree: The LORD said to me, "You are my Son; today I have begotten you. Ask of me, and I will make the nations your heritage, and the ends of the earth your possession. You shall break them with a rod of iron and dash them in pieces like a potter's vessel." (Psalm 2:7-9 ESV)

The dragon could not do any harm to the child until the mission of the "seed of the woman" (the seed from Eve) was accomplished; and He was caught up to God and to His throne. Hebrews 1st Chapter records this majestic truth.

"Who being the brightness of his glory, and the express image of his person, and upholding all things by the word of his power, when he had by himself purged our sins, sat down on the right hand of the Majesty on high" (Hebrews 1:3)

Lord Jesus Christ will come again and will rule from the throne of David. We, the believers in Christ in this church age, will be "caught up" to be with the Lord forever and ever. What a blessing it is to be conformed to the image of Lord Jesus Christ. Bible promises that whoever believes Jesus as the Lord, and believes in heart that God raised him from the dead will be conformed to His image,

"For the Lord himself will descend from heaven with a cry of command, with the voice of an archangel, and with the sound of the trumpet of God. And the dead in Christ will rise first. Then we who are alive, who are left, will be caught up together with them in the clouds to meet the Lord in the air, and so we will always be with the Lord" (1 Thessalonians 4:16-17 ESV)

CHAPTER 38
THE WOMAN, THE MAN CHILD AND THE DRAGON PART II

(FROM REVELATION CHAPTER 12)

SCRIPTURE INTERPRETS SCRIPTURE

The woman escapes all the harm that the dragon intended to bring upon her. God protects her for time, times and half-time and nourishes in the safe place in the wilderness. Virgin Mary is not the woman referred to in Revelation 12 because the woman in this chapter was pregnant.

The Church is chaste virgin espoused to Lord Jesus Christ. The woman referred to cannot be the Church because the scripture says Jesus is the "seed of the woman", and He crushes the seed of the serpent. The Church came into being from Lord Jesus Christ and not the other way round. The seed of the woman will bruise the head of the serpent, which is the devil, also called dragon, or Satan (cf. Rev 12:9).

Jesus was the seed of the woman i.e. He was incarnate God born of the Virgin Mary who was from the lineage of the "Woman" Eve. Satan is rebelled angel. The child is the seed of the woman. John 2:4 and John 19:26 record that Jesus was calling his earthly mother as the "Woman" indicating that He was the seed of the woman. The prophecy recorded in Genesis 3:15 is fulfilled in Lord Jesus Christ, who was the "seed of the woman".

"When Israel was a child, then I loved him, and called my son out of Egypt" (Hosea 11:1)

Abraham's lineage continued through the promised child Isaac and Jacob as recorded in Genesis 17:21. Jacob was chosen and Esau was hated by God. The prophecy recorded in Psalm 2:9 and Revelation 2:27 will be fulfilled at the second coming of Lord Jesus Christ.

"Thou shalt break them with a rod of iron; thou shalt dash them in pieces like a potter's vessel" (Psalms 2:9)

"And he shall rule them with a rod of iron; as the vessels of a potter shall they be broken to shivers: even as I received of my Father" (Revelation 2:27)

In Exodus 4:22 the LORD identified Jacob, who was renamed as "Israel" as His firstborn"

"And thou shalt say unto Pharaoh, Thus saith the LORD, Israel is my son, even my firstborn" (Exodus 4:22)

Apostle Paul wrote as follows: "They are Israelites, and to them belong the adoption, the glory, the covenants, the giving of the law, the worship, and the promises. To them belong the patriarchs, and from their race, according to the flesh, is the Christ, who is God over all, blessed forever. Amen." (Romans 9:4-5 ESV)

CHAPTER 39
THE WOMAN, THE MAN CHILD AND THE DRAGON PART III

(FROM REVELATION CHAPTER 12)

INFERENCE

Study of these scriptures will reveal that the woman referred to in Revelation Chapter 12 is "Israel", the man Child is Lord Jesus Christ, and the Dragon is Satan"

The crux of the problem is that "Replacement Theology" promotes in believing that the Church has replaced Israel and inherited the blessings of Israel. Another problem was from the Reformation Church that ignored eschatology and promoted the beliefs taught by the early Church fathers who believed in Amillennialism. They concentrated more on the Salvation by faith and ignored eschatology.

Israel and the Church are neither one nor the Church is a replacement of Israel. They are both two distinct entities in the sight of God. Jews and Gentiles are made equal in the sight of the Lord and those who believed in Lord Jesus Christ as their Savior have become the "One New Man" (cf. Eph. 2:15).

There were several opportunities given for the children of Israel to believe in Jesus as their Messiah, but they refused to accept Jesus as their Messiah. This resulted in God causing blindness to fall upon Israel that they may not perceive what they see, and that they may not believe that Jesus is their Messiah, until the fullness of Gentiles is come in. All those who believe in Lord

Jesus Christ are part of the Church, and yet they who do not believe in Him will become remnant on the earth.

Even though Israel stumbled and went astray from God, they were restored by God time and again after chastisement because His promises, covenants and blessings for Israel were un-conditional. God made an un-conditional covenant with Abraham and the promised child of Abraham was Isaac.

Apostle Paul deals writes in Romans Chapters 9-11 that God is not through yet with Israel. The Church is in the intermediate position between Israel's blindness of the truth that Lord Jesus Christ is the Messiah and the restoration of Israel. The Church was never revealed in the Old Testament and it was a mystery until it came into being when the Holy Spirit, the promise of the Father, came into the world to indwell the believers in Christ.

If the woman is considered as the Church, the whole scripture about the church being the chaste virgin tumbles down. The woman in the Old Testament scriptures is considered as in travail (cf. Isaiah 54:5; 66:7; Jer.4:31, Micah 4:10; 5:2-3)

There are four women referred to in Revelation and they are (1) Jezebel in 2 Kings 9:10; Rev.2:20; (2) the woman in Rev. Ch.12:1-2 (3); the great whore or the harlot in Rev. 17: 1, 5; 18:2-3; (4) and the Lamb's wife (Rev.19:7; 21:2,9-10)

The woman referred to in Rev. 12 is shown as the one in pregnancy and later giving birth to a man-child. Obviously, the woman cannot be the "Church" because the church is virgin is espoused to Lord Jesus Christ and will be married after the church is "caught up" when the Lord descends from heaven.

"For I feel a divine jealousy for you, since I betrothed you to one husband, to present you as a pure virgin to Christ" (2 Corinthians 11:2 ESV)

The Dragon is the old serpent, who is also called as the Devil, and the Satan, deceived Adam and Eve in the Garden of Eden. It is to be noted that God waged war against Satan and not Satan against God. Satan envied man as his rival and deceived him in the Garden of Eden and took possession of the earth.

However, man and the earth will be redeemed from the bondage of Satan. Lord Jesus bought man by His precious blood shed on the cross. Everyone who confesses that Jesus is Lord and God raised Him from the dead will be saved and will have everlasting life. Revelation 19:11-21; Rev. 21:1; Isaiah 65:17 and 66:22 corroborate the fact that the earth will be redeemed by the power of the Lord.

"The LORD God said to the serpent, 'Because you have done this, cursed are you above all livestock and above all beasts of the field; on your belly you shall go, and dust you shall eat all the days of your life. I will put enmity between you and the woman, and between your offspring and her offspring; he shall bruise your head, and you shall bruise his heel.'"(Genesis 3:14-15 ESV)

"And he laid hold on the dragon, that old serpent, which is the Devil, and Satan, and bound him a thousand years" (Revelation 20:2)

The actions in detail of the Dragon are found in Rev. 12:1-17; 13:1-18; 16:1-21; and Rev. 20:1-15.

CHAPTER 40
THE WOMAN, THE MAN CHILD AND THE DRAGON PART IV

(FROM REVELATION CHAPTER 12)

SALVATION

There was war in heaven. Michael and his angels fought against the dragon. The dragon with all his angels fought back but could not defeat Michael and his angels and, therefore, the dragon did not find any place in heaven.

The great dragon was cast out, and this great dragon was that old serpent, which was the Devil and Satan, who deceived Adam and Eve and presently deceiving the whole world. The dragon with his angels was cast out into the earth.

Note here that the Dragon deceived man already and man fell from the presence of God and yet the dragon which is Satan has access to heaven. Satan had access to heaven when he with his angels presented before the Lord who said to him if he had seen righteous Job. Then, Satan blamed God saying He had put a hedge around him, and therefore, he could not test him. The LORD gave permission to test Job, except to touch his soul. Satan lost the argument and Job was blessed. This was past. Satan is presently deceiving mankind.

Now, when the dragon lost the fight against Michael, the archangel of the LORD, he was cast out of heaven no more to have access there. This is future.

John heard a loud voice saying in heaven, "Now is come salvation, and strength, and the kingdom of our God, and the power of his Christ: for the accuser of our brethren is cast down, which accused them before our God day and night".

The mankind, which believed in Lord Jesus Christ, is saved by the blood of the Lamb and by the word of their testimony and they loved not to live their lives unto death.

The suggestion thereafter is for heaven to rejoice and those dwelling in heaven to rejoice.

Apostle Paul brings a marvelous truth that we the believers in Christ are blessed spiritually and are placed in heavenly places.

"Blessed be the God and Father of our Lord Jesus Christ, who has blessed us in Christ with every spiritual blessing in the heavenly places," (Ephesians 1:3 ESV)

While the heaven rejoices because Satan is cast out of heaven there is a woe proclaimed to the earth-dwellers because the devil, who is full of wrath, is come down to the earth to deceive and trouble them. Satan knows that his time is short.

The dragon having been cast out of heaven tries to persecute the woman, who is representation of Israel, who brought forth Lord Jesus Christ, who is the "seed of the woman". God gives the children of Israel provisions to fly from persecutions of the devil to a safe place in the wilderness and be nourished there for three and half years.

When the serpent seas that the children of Israel were protected in the wilderness it casts out from his mouth water as a flood after the children of Israel that he might cause them to be carried away by the flood.

However, earth helps Israel and opens up her mouth and swallows up the flood that was cast by the dragon from his mouth after the woman. The dragon was wroth with Israel, and went to make war with the remnant of her seed that kept the commandments of God. The remnant, here are Gentiles, who had the testimony of Jesus Christ.

Lord Jesus Christ became sacrifice on behalf of us and fulfilled the Law. He entered into not into Holy place made with hands but into heaven. The Original Ark of the Covenant and the Sanctuary are in Heaven. The Tabernacle built by Moses was a replica of the original sanctuary in heaven.

CHRIST IS OUR HIGH PRIEST

"For Christ has entered, not into holy places made with hands, which are copies of the true things, but into heaven itself, now to appear in the presence of God on our behalf. Nor was it to offer himself repeatedly, as the high priest enters the holy places every year with blood not his own, for then he would have had to suffer repeatedly since the foundation of the world. But as it is, he has appeared once for all at the end of the ages to put away sin by the sacrifice of himself. And just as it is appointed for man to die once, and after that comes judgment, so Christ, having been offered once to bear the sins of many, will appear a second time, not to deal with sin but to save those who are eagerly waiting for him" (Hebrews 9:24-28 ESV)

CHAPTER 41
THE TWO BEASTS (PART I)

(From Revelation 13:1-10)

THE FIRST BEAST (ANTICHRIST)

INTRODUCTION

"And I stood upon the sand of the sea, and saw a beast rise up out of the sea, having seven heads and ten horns, and upon his horns ten crowns, and upon his heads the name of blasphemy" (Revelation 13:1)

The dragon that gave its seat, authority and power to the first beast did not just come up in this chapter, but it was there in the Garden of Eden; but then, who was that dragon and who these two beasts are?

Imagery generally impresses people but in some cases imagery causes confusion. An angel seen in pictures as a woman with pleasant face in white clothes and with beautiful wings is not only an impressive figure for children but also adults. At the same when Satan is presented as a man with horrible face with eyes wide open, painted in red and black colors, and with two horns projecting from his head with his tongue stretched out projects a view as if Satan has bad features. No, Satan indeed wants us to think that he is horrible to look at; but in fact, he comes like an angel of light as Paul writes in 2 Corinthians 11:14 and sometimes as like a roaring lion (cf. 1 Peter 5:8). Satan is cunning, crafty and he is deceiver.

Antichrist and False Prophet are presented as two beasts in Revelation 13 and such imagery as beasts serves similar purpose. They are indeed more dangerous than they are presented as.

John speaks of antichrist in his letters and yet he does not mention the term "antichrist" even once in the book of Revelation. The meaning of "Anti" is "against". He is the one who works against Christ. However, there is much more in the words of Apostle Paul in 2 Thessalonians and John's words in the book of Revelation.

Antichrist who blasphemes the name of God is revealed only after the Church is removed from the earth. This man is the "man of sin" who is also called the "son of perdition".

The serpent, which is also called the 'dragon', was craftier than any other beast of the field that the Lord God made. He enticed woman into sweet talk in the Garden of Eden and used a very pleasing yet cunning phrase and that was "Did God actually say, 'you shall not eat of any tree in the garden'?

The woman may have been taken aback at this question; but she yielded to Satan and said "We may eat of the fruit of the trees in the garden, but God said, 'You shall not eat of the fruit of the tree that is in the midst of the garden, neither shall you touch it, lest you die.'". But the serpent said to the woman, "You will not surely die" and continued cheating her. The woman not only ate the forbidden fruit but she also gave it to man, who also ate and thus both transgressed the command of God (cf. Genesis 3:1-5 ESV)

By one man's sin we are all made sinners and unless we are redeemed from our sin we cannot even see the kingdom of

God. Ever since man fell from the presence of God, there is a constant conflict between the "seed of the woman" and the "seed of the serpent". Redemption of mankind from the bondage of sin under Satan commenced in Genesis Chapter 3:21 and from then onwards man struggles to escape from the temptations from Satan.

It is only by the cleansing of our sin in the blood of Jesus Christ that we will have our salvation and whosoever confesses Jesus Christ as Lord, and believes in heart that God raised Him from the dead will be saved and will have everlasting life.

Lord Jesus Christ, who is the "seed of the woman", defeated the "seed of the serpent" at the cross by offering himself on the cross on behalf of us and paved the way for our salvation. In spite of making provisions for receiving salvation free of cost man has been constantly refusing to accept Jesus Christ as Savior.

The Church was a mystery in the Old Testament period and it came into being with Holy Spirit coming into this world on the Pentecost day to dwell in the hearts of all those who are saved; and all the saved ones are part of the Church. Jesus promised that the gates of hell shall not prevail against the Church and the Church will be protected from the "Great Tribulation".

Out of 70 weeks of Daniel's 70-week prophecy 69 have been completed and the seventieth is yet to come. Immediately after the fullness of the gentiles is come in, as Paul wrote in Romans 11:25 the Church will be removed from this earth the seventieth week begins. After the Church is 'caught up' to be with the Lord forever and ever, the "man of sin" who is also called "son of perdition" will be revealed. He rules peacefully for 3 ½ years and breaks his covenant and persecutes people.

Two times the word "after this" is used in Rev. 4:1. After the seven letters were written to the Churches, and before the throne in heaven was shown to John. Historically the seventh church, which is Laodiceans Church, is the present age. The events that follow after this are recorded from Rev. Ch.4 onwards. There is a clear interval seen between verse 5 and 6 of Rev. Ch.12.

"She gave birth to a male child, one who is to rule all the nations with a rod of iron, but her child was caught up to God and to his throne. (Revelation 12:5 ESV)

"and the woman fled into the wilderness, where she has a place prepared by God, in which she is to be nourished for 1,260 days" (Revelation 12:6 ESV)

THE RISING OF THE FIRST BEAST

Revelation Chapter 13 presents us with the details of two beasts; one rising out of the sea, and other rising from the earth. It is necessary that we understand who these two beasts are. They are two distinct beasts and yet they work together for the common good for the benefit of their head, which is the dragon also called Satan. Thus they form a satanic trinity.

First it is about the first beast. It is not necessary to get disturbed at the symbolism presented in this chapter or any other chapter in Revelation. It could be taken as symbolism or real. If donkey can speak to Balaam and the latter could understand what the donkey spoke to him, the language of the beast also could be understood by the people living during those days, when the beast comes on to the scene.

It is imperative that we recollect the dream that Nebuchadnezzar and Daniel saw and the interpretation of the dreams by Daniel.

Nebuchadnezzar saw in his dream a mighty image and according to Daniel's interpretation he was the mighty image (cf. Daniel 2:31-35). The appearance of the image was frightening. He was the head which was of gold and represented the first kingdom.

Next, his chest and arms in the image, which were of silver, was the second kingdom, inferior to his kingdom, the third part of the image was of his thighs which were made of bronze, which ruled the entire world, and the fourth part of the image was the last kingdom, partly of iron and partly of clay. It was weak because its feet and toes were made of potter's clary and partly or iron.

"And after threescore and two weeks shall Messiah be cut off, but not for himself: and the people of the prince that shall come shall destroy the city and the sanctuary; and the end thereof shall be with a flood, and unto the end of the war desolations are determined" (Daniel 9:26)

The fourth kingdom will be a divided one; one partly strong and the other partly brittle. First one is of the terrible beast, and the second one is of the ten kings and their ten crowns and seven mountains. (cf. Daniel 2:31-43; Rev. 13:1)

In Luke 21:24 Jesus predicts the destruction of Jerusalem and the trampling of the city by the Gentiles and His prediction turned out to be true when after sixty-nine weeks of the Daniel's seventy weeks prophecy He (Messiah) was cut-off and the people of the prince came and destroyed the temple at

Jerusalem, and levelled the whole city of Jerusalem to the ground.

These four kingdoms, as history presents to us the facts, are: Babylon, Persia, Greece, and Roman Empire I (of iron) and II (of iron + clay). Final victory will be of the God of heavens, whose kingdom shall not break but will stand forever.

"And in the days of these kings shall the God of heaven set up a kingdom, which shall never be destroyed: and the kingdom shall not be left to other people, but it shall break in pieces and consume all these kingdoms, and it shall stand for ever" Daniel 2:44

Daniel's vision in Daniel 7:23 corresponds with the vision of Nebuchadnezzar's in Daniel 2:44. He interpreted his dream and finally said:

"Thus he said, The fourth beast shall be the fourth kingdom upon earth, which shall be diverse from all kingdoms, and shall devour the whole earth, and shall tread it down, and break it in pieces" Daniel 7:23

"Now that being broken, whereas four stood up for it, four kingdoms shall stand up out of the nation, but not in his power" Daniel 8:22

From Revelation17:9 it is understood that the seven heads are seven mountains. Horns always represented the power, and here ten horns represent ten kings. This is yet future. A ten-nation federation is going to be formed, and then after their time another shall rise and that is the one who is called "Antichrist" or Pseudo-Christ, "man of sin" or "son of perdition". In Daniel's vision he is referred to as the "little horn"

"I considered the horns, and behold, there came up among them another horn, a little one, before which three of the first horns were plucked up by the roots. And behold, in this horn were eyes like the eyes of a man, and a mouth speaking great things" (Daniel 7:8 ESV)

"As for the ten horns, out of this kingdom ten kings shall arise, and another shall arise after them; he shall be different from the former ones, and shall put down three kings.   He shall speak words against the Most High, and shall wear out the saints of the Most High, and shall think to change the times and the law; and they shall be given into his hand for a time, times, and half a time. But the court shall sit in judgment, and his dominion shall be taken away, to be consumed and destroyed to the end. (Daniel 7:24-26 ESV)

"Out of one of them came a little horn, which grew exceedingly great toward the south, toward the east, and toward the glorious land" (Daniel 8:9 ESV)

John saw a beast rising up out of the sea, having seven heads and ten horns, and upon his horns were ten crowns, which were "diadems", and not "stephanos". Diadems are ornamental crowns worn by the kings which stephanos are earned by athletes. And, again from Rev. 17:12 it is understood that the ten horns are ten kings.

John saw in his vision the first beast whose appearance was eccentric and horrible. It had ten horns and seven heads, with ten diadems on its horns. One of its seven heads suffered a deadly wound, perhaps as a result of a scathing attack made on it; however, this mortal wound was healed.

Marvelous as the healing was, the earth-dwellers are surprised and taken into false belief that he is the Christ. They will be deceived and follow him and worship him. Paul writes in 2 Thessalonians 2:10-11 that because they received not the love of the truth God sends them into strong delusion that they believe in a lie.

"And with all deceivableness of unrighteousness in them that perish; because they received not the love of the truth, that they might be saved. And for this cause God shall send them strong delusion, that they should believe a lie" (2 Thessalonians 2:10-11)

They who refused to worship the living God saying there is no God then seek to refuge in the beast and worship it. Psalmist wrote in Psalm 14:1a that "The fool hath said in his heart, There is no God". They not only worship the beast but flatter it and praise it saying "Who is like the beast, and who can fight against it?"

This first beast looks like a leopard but its feet were like a bear's; and its mouth was like a lion's mouth. Even though it has lion's mouth and the power to utter blasphemous words its boasting mouth was limited to a period of forty two months. It does not speak words devoid of meaning, but it speaks haughty and blasphemous words. It does not speak the words of men or against men, but speaks blasphemy against God, blaspheming His name and His dwelling and of those who dwell in heaven.

Apostle Paul speaks of this 'man of sin', the son of perdition' in 2 Thessalonians chapter 2:1-17. The 'man of sin' receives such great power that he puts to death the two witnesses who had the power to call fire from heaven and swallow anyone who tried to hurt them. (cf. Revelation Ch. 11:3-19)

The situation in that period will be so pathetic that even the saints in this period are conquered by the beast. he saints of this "great tribulation" period are not protected. If it were to be in the Church period, the beast could not do any harm to the saints in Christ because Lord Jesus said, the gates of hell will not prevail against the Church; and the Church period is here now. Do not let your soul go into "great tribulation" period.

The beast is given authority over every tribe and people and languages and nation. Every one, of all the earth-dwellers, whose name is not written in the "book of life of the lamb", will worship it.

Lord Jesus Christ, who was identified twice by John the Baptist as the "Lamb of God", was slain on behalf of us on the cross in order that sinners may by confessing Him as the Lord, and by believing that God raised Him from the dead receive everlasting life to be with Him forever and ever conformed to His image and in glorified bodies.

However, those who preferred to refuse Him as the Messiah become remnant to be as earth-dwellers with mortal bodies still suffering pain and sufferings, sickness and worship the beast, finally to be thrown into 'lake of fire' along with the beast.

Who can be against the Almighty God or speak against the living God? Just as the beast speaks blasphemous words for limited period some also speak, either in their ignorance, or in arrogance that there is no God, and end up in unimaginable misery. They have no hope of their life after their death. They prefer to enjoy worldly pleasures now and say, "we will see after death", but when it comes to happen it would have been very late.

Patience calls for it and the saints are comforted that they should not take up sword for sword. Vengeance belongs to God and persecutors will not escape punishment from the living God.

"If anyone is to be taken captive, to captivity he goes; if anyone is to be slain with the sword, with the sword must he be slain. Here is a call for the endurance and faith of the saints" (Revelation 13:9-10 ESV)

CHAPTER 42
THE TWO BEASTS (PART II)

(From Revelation 13:11-18)

THE RISING OF THE SECOND BEAST: FALSE PROPHET

"I considered the horns, and, behold, there came up among them another little horn, before whom there were three of the first horns plucked up by the roots: and, behold, in this horn were eyes like the eyes of man, and a mouth speaking great things" (Daniel 7:8)

Daniel saw in his vision the same pattern that Nebuchadnezzar saw in his vision. The four kingdoms that follow one after another giving way finally to the last government by a human being, who would have power for a limited duration, and who speaks great words of blaspheme. However, the final victory is of our Lord Jesus Christ, who establishes literal Kingdom of God.

"I looked then because of the sound of the great words that the horn was speaking. And as I looked, the beast was killed, and its body destroyed and given over to be burned with fire. As for the rest of the beasts, their dominion was taken away, but their lives were prolonged for a season and a time" (Daniel 7:11-12 ESV)

Jesus warned His disciples to be careful of many who shall come in His name saying "I am Christ; and shall deceive many".

"And Jesus answered and said unto them, Take heed that no man deceive you. For many shall come in my name, saying, I am Christ; and shall deceive many" (Matthew 24:4-5)

John in his vision saw the first beast coming out of sea and the second beast coming out of the earth. The second beast represents false prophet, who exalts the first beast ('man of sin'), and commends him to people to worship of the first beast, which suffered a fatal wound and yet survived.

The ultimate goal of Antichrist and the false prophet is to bring glory to Satan and to cause people to worship the dragon, also called Satan the old serpent, which deceived Adam and Eve in the Garden of Eden. False prophet's main work is to gather people into Satan's fold and identify them as belonging to Satan. This is intolerable sin in the sight of the LORD, and the destiny of those who do such heinous act will be "lake of fire"

"And the beast was taken, and with him the false prophet that wrought miracles before him, with which he deceived them that had received the mark of the beast, and them that worshipped his image. These both were cast alive into a lake of fire burning with brimstone" (Revelation 19:20)

Repeated mention of the wound the first beast suffered, and the healing of it, shows that there is much significance attached to it. The healing is seen as a miracle and an act of act of god. The presence of the wound gives credence to Antichrist that he is god, thus exalting Satan above all. The second beast helps in bringing glory to the first beast, which in turn brings glory to Satan. The healed wound becomes an authentic sign for it to deceive people and to cause people to worship the first beast.

The second beast has two horns like a lamb and comes out of the earth and speaks like a dragon. The two horns would be to show that he is a political leader and a religious leader as well. He does great miracles in the presence of the first beast. It causes the earth and its inhabitants worship the first beast, whose mortal wound was healed.

The second beast performs great signs and wonders such as those performed by the two witnesses. The two witnesses had the power to bring fire from their mouth and consumed anyone who attempted to hurt them. Similar are the powers that the second beast wields.

It is interesting to note that Satan is a good imitator and his agents did miracles similar to the ones that Moses did. However, the magicians of Satan could not do all the miracles that Moses and Aaron, the servants of God, did nor could they prevail before them. Moses threw the rod in his hands and it turned serpent. The magicians threw the rods in their hands and they too turned serpents, but the rod which became serpent from Moses' hand swallowed the serpents that Magicians brought forth.

The second beast takes undue advantage of partial knowledge of people and makes them to worship the first beast. Every man has an innate longing to worship something; may be God; or man; or an inanimate object; and when he refuses to understand the value of the free gift of salvation the true God has given, he tends to worship a man or inanimate object.

It is so sad that even though the truth is revealed to man, yet he prefers to worship a man who comes as god instead of worshipping the God who created heavens and the earth. To such persons who refuse the truth, God rewards them a strong delusion that they may believe a lie as truth and embrace falsehood and live by it. They see miracles from men as the real ones from the true God and are misled.

"And even as they did not like to retain God in their knowledge, God gave them over to a reprobate mind, to do those things which are not convenient" (Romans 1:28)

John saw that the second beast caused people to worship the first beast and whoever did not worship the first beast was slain. The second beast was allowed even to give breath to the image of the first beast and make it to speak. That is how Antichrist exalts himself as god and forces people to worship him. False prophet causes rich and poor, free and slave, small and great to be marked on the right hand or the forehead his number which is 666 and those that did not have that number could not sell or buy any merchandize.

The number 666 referred to here is not something that we find on bar-codes and microchips, but it is the number of man; basically saying that Antichrist is a man and not a god. In scriptures man's number is identified as 6; man is imperfect and is created on the sixth day.

Bible prohibits tattooing or making any marks or cuts on the body. If anyone gets the mark 666 on his/her body it is a clear identification that he/she belongs to Satan. Because he/she identifies that he belongs to Satan, there is no salvation for him/her, and he/she is lost forever. Never either in this age or in the age to come anyone should get this identification of Antichrist's number, 666.

"You shall not make any cuts on your body for the dead or tattoo yourselves: I am the LORD" (Leviticus 19:28 ESV)

Bible tells all of us to have wisdom and understand that the number of the beast is 666 and it is man's number. The scripture is for us to understand clearly that the man who exalts proclaiming that he is god, and sits in temple and cause sacrifices and oblations to cease is a mere man. Antichrist, false prophet and Satan will finally be cast into "lake of fire" (cf. Daniel 9:27; Matt. 24: 4-5; 2 Thess. 2:3-11;Rev.13:1-18).

"Here is wisdom. Let him that hath understanding count the number of the beast: for it is the number of a man; and his number is Six hundred threescore and six" (Revelation 13:18)

"And the devil that deceived them was cast into the lake of fire and brimstone, where the beast and the false prophet are, and shall be tormented day and night for ever and ever" (Revelation 20:10)

Many of us, who have received salvation free of cost, take it for granted that we received salvation because of our merit without realizing the price that was paid for our salvation. The price was paid by Lord Jesus Christ and the price was not silver or gold, but His blood. We are saved by grace through faith; not by our good works. There is going to be "great tribulation such as was not since the beginning of the world to this time, no, nor shall ever be"

"For then shall be great tribulation, such as was not since the beginning of the world to this time, no, nor ever shall be". (Matthew 24:21)

Antichrist will kill those who do not worship him; people will not be able to buy merchandize without his number, which is 666, on the right hand or the forehead. There is only one hope and it is now here. Confess your sins to Jesus and accept Jesus Christ as the Lord of your life and believe in your heart that God raised Him from the dead.

"for all have sinned and fall short of the glory of God, and are justified by his grace as a gift, through the redemption that is in Christ Jesus, whom God put forward as a propitiation by his blood, to be received by faith. This was to show God's righteousness, because in his divine forbearance he had passed over former sins" (Romans 3:23-25 ESV)

CHAPTER 43
SICKLE AND HARVEST (PART I)

(From Revelation 14:1-5)

THE LAMB AND THE 144,000

"Then I looked, and behold, on Mount Zion stood the Lamb, and with him 144,000 who had his name and his Father's name written on their foreheads" (Revelation 14:1 ESV)

MOUNT ZION

Mount Zion is the region comprising of Jerusalem, which is the city of David, and surrounding areas. Many times Zion is mentioned in the Bible to refer to Jerusalem and surrounding areas; sometimes in parallelism with Jerusalem or sometimes specially to refer Jerusalem alone. (In Parallelism cf. Ps 102:21; Am 1:2; Mic 3:10, 12; Zech. 1:14, 17; 8:3; Zep 3:16) or (in specific cases; Jer. 3:14; La 5:11).

John saw in his vision Lord Jesus Christ standing on Mount Zion and with him were 144,000, who had His name and Father's name written on their foreheads. There are three facts mentioned in this chapter which serves as Table of Contents of the seven bowls to come in.

1. Firstly, it is about 144,000
2. Secondly, it is about angels (Three with proclamations and three with call for "Grape Harvest")
3. Thirdly, it is about harvesting.

ABOUT 144,000

God chose 12,000 children of Israel from each of the twelve tribes and sealed them for redemption and this occurs during "Great Tribulation" period. These 144,000, who John saw in his vision as sealed and redeemed from the earth and from mankind as first-fruits for the Father and the Son. They were first seen in Revelation Chapter 7, and are distinct from the twenty four elders, who are representatives of the Church.

The name of "Dan" does not figure in the list mentioned in Revelation Chapter 7 probably because the tribe of "Dan" was the first one who adopted idolatry at the northern border of Israel. However, it is pleasing to note that his name is mentioned in the portion allotted to him in Ezekiel 48:1-35. Another point to be noted is that although the name of tribe of Ephraim is not mentioned, his name was taken indirectly as the tribe of Joseph, and Manasseh's name is mentioned separately. The low profiling of Ephraim may also be because it is from the tribe of Manasseh that idolatry did spread in Northern Kingdom of Israel.

Jews and Gentiles, who are redeemed by the blood of Jesus Christ have become "One New Man" in Christ and will be "caught up" to be with the Lord forever and ever. The Church is the bride of Christ. While the salvation of 144,000 is also achieved by the blood of Jesus Christ they go through the "great tribulation" period because they did not accept Jesus as their savior during the Church age.

The 144,000 children of Israel sealed for redemption are not in heaven; neither did Lord Jesus descend physically yet onto Mount of Olives when John saw the vision. The second advent Lord Jesus Christ on the earth will be after the second half of seventieth week of Daniel's 70-week prophecy (that is after the 3 ½ years "Great Tribulation" period). Obviously, the 144,000 were seen in John's vision, as they would be with Jesus, on the Mount Olives when He steps on it.

"Having abolished in his flesh the enmity, even the law of commandments contained in ordinances; for to make in himself of twain one new man, so making peace" (Ephesians 2:15)

The 144,000 are redeemed in "Great Tribulation" period and they follow the bride and the bridegroom like friends. They are not part of bride or the bridegroom. We who belong to the Church "are caught up" to be with Lord Jesus Christ forever and ever, and are confirmed to His image when we see Lord Jesus Christ coming in the clouds.

The beast mentioned in Revelation 13 makes war against saints in "Great Tribulation" period and overcomes them. All those who do not worship the beast will be slain (cf. Rev. 13:7); but it had no power over 144,000, who are given the seal of protection on their foreheads.

Satan is good imitator as seen in copying the pattern from God by sealing those who belong to him with 666 and thus all those who have the "mark of the beast" are of him. Reader should better decide whether he wants to be with the Lord without entering into the "Great Tribulation" period, or enter and pass through tribulation many times over than that of the present period.

The beast is given power to conquer the saints in that period, and it is only those who endure his persecution, and be slain, for the Lord will be saved. To enjoy the privilege of not being persecuted by Antichrist the best time to repent of sins, and receive everlasting life, is now.

There was a voice from heaven like many waters roaring with sound of loud thunder. The voice was like the sound of harpists playing on their haps. They all sang a new song before the throne and before the living creatures and before the elders. Except for the 144,000 redeemed children of Israel no one could learn that song.

The 144,000 had not defiled themselves with women and they were all male virgins. The term "Virgin" not only used for females who have not defiled their chastity but also used for males who have not defiled their chastity with women. Some believe that this verse does not speak of their physical purity but of spiritually purity; however, the text mentions that they have not defiled with women and we understand as the text says.

There is *no* lie found in their mouths and they are blameless and they follow Lord Jesus Christ wherever He goes. It is hard for someone to be without lying or being blameless, but these 144,000 are surely, as the text says, without any blame and did not lie.

Bible does not say that the blindness has fallen on all the children of Israel but it says blindness *in part* is happened to Israel, and that is the reason why we see many Jews, who have accepted Jesus as their personal savior, are working for the Lord and His kingdom.

"For I would not, brethren, that ye should be ignorant of this mystery, lest ye should be wise in your own conceits; that blindness in part is happened to Israel, until the fullness of the Gentiles be come in" (Romans 11:25)

CHAPTER 44
SICKLE AND HARVEST (PART II)

(From Revelation 14:6-13)

THE MESSAGES OF ANGELS

God gave responsibility to his disciples to preach the Gospel of Jesus Christ and every believer in Christ proclaims His message to the extent possible. Jesus said "this gospel of the kingdom will be proclaimed throughout the whole world as a testimony to all nations, and then the end will come" (Matthew 24:14 ESV)

Notice the words of Lord Jesus, who said "this gospel of the kingdom"; obviously He was speaking in reference to the Gospel that the angel would preach to the earth-dwellers during 'great tribulation' period.

Lord Jesus Christ gave commission to His disciples to "teach all nations, baptizing them in the name of the Father, and of the Son, and of the Holy Ghost: Teaching them to observe all things whatsoever I have commanded you: and, lo, I am with you alway, even unto the end of the world. Amen". (Matthew 28:19-20).

He said to them that "they shall receive power, after Holy Spirit came upon them, and they shall be witness unto Him in Jerusalem, and in all Judea, and in Samaria, and uttermost part of the earth" (cf. Acts 1:8)

The disciples of Jesus Christ preached, the Gospel of Jesus Christ, mainly to the areas where the children of Israel were scattered, and the Gospel was heard by others as well. Apostle

Paul was made a minister to preach the Gospel to the Gentiles. He preached, in his missionary itineraries, first to the Jews and then to the Gentiles from Jerusalem to Rome and then he declared that Gospel was preached to every creature which is under heaven (cf. Colossians 1:6; 1:23; Romans 1:8; Galatians 1:17; Romans 15:19; Romans 15:24-28).

As Jews continued to reject Jesus as their Messiah, and in order that the Gentiles may receive salvation, God allowed blindness in part to happen to Israel until the fullness of the Gentiles is come in. (cf. Romans 11:25)

In spite of preaching the message of Salvation to the whole world by various methods of available network communications, many Jews and Gentiles still refuse to accept Jesus as their savior, or hear the Gospel. That is the reason why even at the time of "rapture" of the Church there is remnant.

The Church, which has taken it as a challenge to preach the Gospel of Grace to all the nations, will not be held responsible for failure to do so to the small tribal unreachable villages; and this reason would not be an obstacle for Lord Jesus to return again. The Church should never be slack in proclaiming the Gospel of Jesus Christ on this pretext. Each individual also will be held responsible inasmuch as there is responsibility on every man to seek God and understand Him (cf. Jeremiah 9:23-24; Habakkuk 2:14).

"Claiming to be wise, they became fools, and exchanged the glory of the immortal God for images resembling mortal man and birds and animals and creeping things. Therefore God gave them up in the lusts of their hearts to impurity, to the dishonoring of their bodies among themselves" (Romans 1:22-24 ESV).

To the remnant that is called as "earth-dwellers", the Gospel is preached by 144,000 of Jewish descendants and many will believe in Christ (cf. Revelation 7:9). There will also be many who will not believe in Christ. This is the time when three angels proclaim, one after another, three important messages.

The first angel flying directly overhead proclaims the eternal gospel to the earth-dwellers in every nation, tribe and language and people. This eternal gospel is not the gospel of grace that we preach, but it is declaration that everyone should "Fear God and give him glory, because the hour of his judgment has come, and worship him who made heaven and earth, the sea and the springs of water." (cf. Rev. 14:6)

"...at the name of Jesus every knee should bow, in heaven and on earth and under the earth, and every tongue confess that Jesus Christ is Lord, to the glory of God the Father" (Philippians 2:10-11 ESV)

The second angel proclaims that "Fallen, fallen is Babylon the great, she who made all nations drink the wine of the passion of her sexual immorality." The repetition of the word "Fallen" emphasizes the intensity with which the Babylon will be destroyed.

The third angel proclaims the seriousness of identifying with the "man of sin" also called the "son of perdition" by receiving his number 666 on forehead or on right hand.

"If anyone worships the beast and its image and receives a mark on his forehead or on his hand, he also will drink the wine of God's wrath, poured full strength into the cup of his anger, and he will be tormented with fire and sulfur in the presence of the holy angels and in the presence of the Lamb. And the smoke of their torment goes up forever and ever, and they have no rest, day or night, these worshipers of the beast and its image, and whoever receives the mark of its name." (Revelation 14:6-11 ESV)

COMFORT

There is no rest either in the day or in the night for the worshippers, who receive the mark of the name of the beast and its image. On the contrary there is perfect rest assured for those who keep the commandments of God and their faith in Jesus. John says he heard a voice from heaven which said to him to write that those who die from then onward are blessed and "Blessed indeed," says the Spirit, "that they may rest from their labors, for their deeds follow them!" (cf. Revelation 14:12-13)

CHAPTER 45
SICKLE AND HARVEST (PART III)

(From Revelation 14:14-20)

THE GRAPE HARVEST

By the time John saw in his vision the angels calling out for harvest it was the time when man was at the peak on his mountain of rebellion against God. Man's rebellion against God started in the Garden of Eden, where woman was deceived by the serpent, and man and woman, who transgressed against God's command, were driven out from the Garden of Eden.

God is longsuffering and patient and, therefore, He has shown His mercy towards man from the beginning; and yet many rejected Him as their Lord in their lives. They rejected "theocracy" which is direct rule from God, His rule over Israel by Judges, His rule over them by kings, and they violated the Ten Commandments. God then sent His only Son into this world to die on behalf of sinners in order that whoever believes in Him shall not perish but have everlasting life.

Man's rebellion against God continued and he said in his heart that there is no God. King David described man's rebellion in his psalm as follows:

"The fool hath said in his heart, There is no God. They are corrupt, they have done abominable works, there is none that doeth good" (Psalms 14:1)

A quick reading of Revelation Chapter 14 gives a false impression that God was going to reap believers from the earth;

but inasmuch as it was not the wheat harvest, the reaping was of the ungodly and rebellious in order to destroy them. The word "ripe" used here was not just the ripen condition of the fruit that one may be able to eat, but it was over-ripe, which is worth for nothing but to be thrown away as garbage for destruction.

"And another angel came out from the altar, which had power over fire; and cried with a loud cry to him that had the sharp sickle, saying, Thrust in thy sharp sickle, and gather the clusters of the vine of the earth; for her grapes are fully ripe" (Revelation 14:18)

John saw in his vision one like the "Son of man", who sat upon the white cloud. He had in his head a golden crown, and in his hand a sharp sickle. Daniel prophesied about the coming of Lord Jesus Christ, whom he identified as the "Son of man" with the clouds of heaven.

"I saw in the night visions, and, behold, one like the Son of man came with the clouds of heaven, and came to the Ancient of days, and they brought him near before him" (Daniel 7:13)

In Revelation Chapter 14:13 there is an assurance that "Blessed are the dead who die in the Lord from now on", which corroborates "Pre-tribulation Rapture" and that is the reason why the assurance here is for those "who die in the Lord from now on" that they are blessed and they will rest from their labors. The Church, which shall be caught up, will be at rest even before those of whom it is spoken of in Revelation 14:13. Paul says in 1 Thessalonians 4:16-17

"For the Lord himself shall descend from heaven with a shout, with the voice of the archangel, and with the trump of God: and the dead in Christ shall rise first: Then we which are alive and remain shall be caught up together with them in the clouds, to meet the Lord in the air: and so shall we ever be with the Lord".

The clouds, as we read at several places in the Old Testament, show the glory of God. The LORD went before the children of Israel "in a pillar of cloud, to lead them the way, and by night in a pillar of fire" (cf. Exodus 13:21).

Moses climbed up the Mount Sinai and the LORD descended in the cloud on to the Mount Sinai and stood with him there and proclaimed His name. Moses made haste and bowed his head toward the earth and worshipped the LORD (cf. Exodus 34:4-8).

The "cloud covered the tent of the congregation, and the glory of the LORD filled the tabernacle" (cf. Exodus 40:34)

The angel said to Mary that "The Holy Ghost shall come upon thee, and the power of the Highest shall overshadow thee: therefore also that holy thing which shall be born of thee shall be called the Son of God" (Luke 1:35)

From these verses it is inferred that the one who sat on the white cloud was Lord Jesus Christ, who had on head a golden crown, a victor's sign, and a sharp sickle. As John saw in his vision this "grape harvest" the Lord was going to reap is yet future in preparation for the "Armageddon war".

And I looked, and behold a white cloud, and upon the cloud one sat like unto the Son of man, having on his head a golden crown, and in his hand a sharp sickle. (Revelation 14:14)

The events that occur before the second coming of Lord Jesus Christ and the divine vengeance are prophesied in Joel 3:13

"Put ye in the sickle, for the harvest is ripe: come, get you down; for the press is full, the fats overflow; for their wickedness is great" (Joel 3:13)

Psalmist asks as to why the heathen rage and the people imagine a vain thing. Can anyone fight against the LORD?

Wise men, mighty kings, princes, and dictators have come and gone. There were mighty men like Sihon the king of Amorites, and Og, the king of Bashan, who faced defeated at the hands of the children of Israel with the help of Almighty God (cf. Numbers 21:21-24). There was Goliath, who was killed by David with the help of God. Such will be the fate of all those who oppose God and His people.

When man takes refuge in his own strength and wisdom the LORD will have him in derision. The Father says He has set Jesus upon the holy hill of Zion. This is a prophecy and it is about the thousand year peaceful reign of our Lord Jesus Christ from the throne of David.

The Father promises that the uttermost parts will be given to The Son for his possession. Jesus is the Son of God and he shall break the mighty men with iron rod and he breaks them as the rod strikes a potter's

"Thou shalt break them with a rod of iron; thou shalt dash them in pieces like a potter's vessel". (Psalms 2:9)

Now, when it was time to reap another angel came out of the temple calling out to the one who sat on the cloud "Put in your sickle, and reap, for the hour to reap has come, for the harvest of the earth is fully ripe."

Interestingly, a question would probably arise if an angel can say to the Lord to do His work such as to reap with sickle. The Lord did not do anything without first praying to the Father, and likewise, it is Father who said to Him that He will give Lord Jesus His inheritance.

"Ask of me, and I shall give thee the heathen for thine inheritance, and the uttermost parts of the earth for thy possession" (Psalms 2:8)

In all possibility it was not an order from an angel; but a signal to go ahead with His plan and/or a request based on the prayers of saints. Man's rebellion and persecution of saints had reached its peak, beyond tolerable limits. Therefore, the one who sat on the cloud swung his sickle across the earth and the earth was reaped.

After that another angel came out of the temple in heaven. He too had a sharp sickle. Then, another angel, who had the authority over the fire, came out of the altar and called out with a loud voice to the one who had sharp sickle, "Put in your sickle and gather the clusters from the vine of the earth, for its grapes are ripe."

The angel swung his sickle across the earth and gathered the grape harvest of the earth and threw these over-ripe grapes it into the great winepress of the wrath of God. The winepress was trodden outside the city, and the wine blew from the winepress and stood up to the height of horse's bridle, which is say four feet high, and up to a distance of 1600 furlongs or 184 miles, which the distance from Megiddo to Petra via Jerusalem.

"Send ye the lamb to the ruler of the land from Sela to the wilderness, unto the mount of the daughter of Zion". (Isaiah

16:1) ("Sela" is the rock city and capital of Edom and it is called as "Petra" cf. 2Ki 14:7; Isa 16:1. In Jg. 1:36; 2Ch 25:12; and Ob 1:3)

"And the winepress was trodden outside the city, and blood flowed from the winepress, as high as a horse's bridle, for 1,600 stadia"

CHAPTER 46
THE BEGINNIG OF THE END

(From Revelation Chapter 15)

THE SEVEN ANGELS WITH SEVEN PLAGUES

"Then I saw another sign in heaven, great and amazing, seven angels with seven plagues, which are the last, for with them the wrath of God is finished" (Revelation 15:1 ESV)

Revelation chapter 15 serves as a prelude to the events that would come shortly hereafter. It is the beginning of the end of wicked earth and the wicked people; the end of old creation; the utter destruction of this wicked world, followed by the new creation. It is the hope of believers in Christ that they will have a blessed life in the new creation; while it is the doom of the unbelievers who will finally end up in the "lake of fire".

Earlier in Chapter 4 John saw flashes of lightning, rumbling and peals of thunder coming forth, and before the throne of God there were seven lamps of fire burning, which are the seven Spirits of God; and before the throne there was a sea of glass like crystal and in the midst of the throne and round about the throne were four living creatures, full of eyes in front and behind.

The sea represents symbolically purity, clear and calmness but in this chapter this 'sea of glass' is mixed with fire, which represents judgment. In Revelation Chapter 8 when the first angel sounded the first trumpet "there followed hail and fire mingled with blood, and they were cast upon the earth: and the third part of trees was burnt up, and all green grass was burnt up. (cf. Revelation 8:7)

John saw another sign in heaven, which was great and marvelous. He saw seven angels having seven last plagues and in them was the wrath of God filled up. The phrase "wrath of God filled up" indicates that it is the culmination point where judgment of the earth and of the earth-dwellers will be met with.

One of the living creatures before God hands over to the seven angels the seven golden bowls (also called 'vials') full of wrath of God, who lives forever and ever. In Revelation Chapter 4 there were seen seven lamps of fire burning before the throne and they were seven Spirits of God. Number seven indicates completeness. Here in this chapter are seen the seven angels with seven bowls filled with the wrath of God. Pouring out of them the plagues, as seen in subsequent chapters, indicates that the wrath of God finishes with that.

"And one of the four living creatures gave to the seven angels seven golden bowls full of the wrath of God who lives forever and ever" (Revelation 15:7 ESV)

There were also seen those who were triumphant over the persecution of the beast, ("man of sin", "the son of perdition"), by refusing to take upon their foreheads or on their right hand the "the mark of the beast", 666, and thereby became martyrs for the Lord (cf. Rev. 7:9-17). They were all standing upon the sea of glass having the harps of God. (cf. Revelation 15:2, 3)

"And they sing the song of Moses, the servant of God, and the song of the Lamb, saying,

Great and amazing are your deeds, O Lord God the Almighty!

Just and true are your ways, O King of the nations!

Who will not fear, O Lord, and glorify your name? For you alone are holy.

All nations will come and worship you, for your righteous acts have been revealed."

(Revelation 15:3-4 ESV)

Moses and the children of Israel sang a song unto the LORD after their crossing over to the other side of the Red Sea on the dry ground in the midst of it, where God drowned Pharaoh and his chasing chariots and his army by gathering waters back once again.

"Then sang Moses and the children of Israel this song unto the LORD, and spake, saying, I will sing unto the LORD, for he hath triumphed gloriously: the horse and his rider hath he thrown into the sea" (Exodus Chapter 15:1)

They praised the mighty works of the LORD. Miriam, his sister, Aaron, his brother played timbrel and danced and all the women followed them.

Miriam said "...Sing ye to the LORD, for he hath triumphed gloriously; the horse and his rider hath he thrown into the sea. (Exodus 15:21)

The blast from the nostrils of the LORD gathered the waters in the Red sea and it split up to stand upright like heap and with the strength like that of a rock on either side of the dry pathway which the LORD made for the children of Israel and their cattle to tread on.

The outstretched and mighty hand of the LORD delivered them from the bondage of slavery and in recognition of God's faithfulness they sang the song. They sang the excellence of the LORD and praised Him and they sang that the enemy pursued them but they were overthrown by the power of God. The pride of the enemy was brought to no effect and God blew the wind over the Red Sea.

The children of Israel walked to their safety under the mighty hands of God beyond the Red Sea and then at the command of God Moses stretched forth his hand over the Red sea and the sea returned to normal. Egyptians tried to escape against the tide of the waters, but the waters covered the chariots, the horsemen, and the entire host of Pharaoh who came pursuing after them. The LORD took off the wheels of their chariots and His right hand was glorious in power and it dashed the enemy into pieces.

The children of Israel continued singing "Who is like unto thee, O LORD, among the gods? who is like thee, glorious in holiness, fearful in praises, doing wonders?" (Cf. Exodus 15:8, 11, Exodus 13:18-22 and 14:24-30) The LORD reigns for ever and ever and He is with us always.

There is reason for us to sing unto the Lord because Jesus paid price for our salvation. It is neither by silver nor by gold or by our good works but by the precious blood of Jesus that we have our salvation. Let us sing unto the LORD as Psalmist sang unto Him when his heart rejoiced in Him.

"O come, let us sing unto the LORD: let us make a joyful noise to the rock of our salvation" (Psalms 95:1)

The song of Moses is also recorded in Exodus 19 before giving of the Law by God, and in Deuteronomy chapter 32 before Moses, the servant of God, ended his life on this earth. The song of the Lamb is recorded in Revelation 5:9

Great and amazing are the deeds of our Lord God the Almighty, who redeemed the children of Israelites from the bondage of slavery under Pharaoh, and us from the bondage of sin by the blood of Lord Jesus Christ. He defeated Sihon the king of Amorites, and Og, the king of Bashan, and the "seed of the serpent" at the cross.

All those refusing to accept Jesus as their savior will one day bow before Him as the scripture says "That at the name of Jesus every knee should bow, of things in heaven, and things in earth, and things under the earth; And that every tongue should confess that Jesus Christ is Lord, to the glory of God the Father" (Philippians 2:10-11)

"Thou art worthy, O Lord, to receive glory and honour and power: for thou hast created all things, and for thy pleasure they are and were created" (Revelation 4:11)

"...Holy, holy, holy, is the LORD of hosts: the whole earth is full of his glory" (Isaiah 6:3)

John emphasizes the eternal nature of Lord Jesus Christ while wishing grace and peace from Him saying,"...who is, and who was, and who is to come" (cf. Revelation 1:4-5)

Jehovah promised to Lord Jesus Christ that He will grant heathen for His inheritance and uttermost parts of the earth for His possession (cf. Psalm 2:8)

The Tabernacle, the Ark of the Covenant that Moses built was replica of the original sanctuary in heaven. John looked and the sanctuary of the tent of witness in heaven was opened, and out of the sanctuary came the seven angels with the seven plagues, clothed in pure, bright linen, with golden sashes around their chests.

The Sanctuary was filled with smoke which indicates the presence of God. No one could enter the sanctuary until the seven plagues from the seven bowls were poured out by the seven angels, one after another, whereby the wrath of God finishes.

Believe in Lord Jesus Christ.

"Neither is there salvation in any other: for there is none other name under heaven given among men, whereby we must be saved" (Acts 4:12)

CHAPTER 47
THE SEVEN BOWLS PART I

(From Revelation 16:1-2, 15)

THE SEVEN BOWLS OF GOD'S WRATH

("Behold, I am coming like a thief! Blessed is the one who stays awake, keeping his garments on, that he may not go about naked and be seen exposed!") (Revelation 16:15 ESV)

Except for verse 15 of this chapter that serves as a parenthesis, all other verses in this chapter deal with the wrath of God. Verse 15 refers to the coming of Lord Jesus Christ in "The Day of the Lord" which surprises those who are in darkness. Very often it is confusing to many that Lord Jesus Christ is going to come as a thief for everyone on the earth; but certainly it is not so.

Apostle Paul makes it clear in 1 Thessalonians 5th chapter that there are two groups of people. He specifies believers in Christ as those who are not in darkness. The believers are the children of light and the children of the day; not of night or of the darkness. But for those who are in darkness and in the night the Lord's coming is like a thief in the night. While people are comfortable saying "'There is peace of and security', then destruction will come upon them as labor pains upon a pregnant woman and they will not escape" (cf. 1 Thessalonians 5:1-11)

Is Paul contradicting Lord Jesus Christ's words in Matthew 24:43?

"But know this that if the master of the house had known in what part of the night the thief was coming, he would have stayed awake and would not have let his house be broken into. Therefore you also must be ready, for the Son of Man is coming at an hour you do not expect" (Matthew 24:43-44 ESV)

No, Paul confirms the words of Lord Jesus Christ and says that we the believers in Christ know that the "day of the Lord will come like a thief in the night". Paul advises believers to be sober, put on the breastplate of faith and love and helmet of salvation inasmuch as God has not destined us to face the wrath of God, but to obtain salvation through Jesus Christ our Lord, who died on behalf of us in order that we may live with him forever and ever. He confirms that we are as much aware of the fact that the "Day of the Lord" will come, as did the disciples of Jesus.

Apostle Peter says that the Lord will come as a thief in the night when the "heavens shall pass away with a great noise, and the elements shall melt with fervent heat, the earth also and the works that are therein shall be burned up" (cf. 2 Peter 3:10). Obviously the wrath of God is poured upon the earth-dwellers after the Church is "caught up".

"For God has not destined us for wrath, but to obtain salvation through our Lord Jesus Christ, who died for us so that whether we are awake or asleep we might live with him" (1 Thessalonians 5:9-10 ESV)

It was a warning to the church in Sardis that "therefore thou shalt not watch, I will come on thee as a thief, and thou shalt not know what hour I will come upon thee" (Revelation 3:3)

In this chapter Lord Jesus Christ details for us through John his servant the wrath of God that will be poured, one after another. The seven angels pour out one bowl each, according to their turn, upon the earth and earth-dwellers, sea, rivers and springs of water, sun, throne of the beast, river Euphrates and the air.

"Then I heard a loud voice from the temple telling the seven angels, 'Go and pour out on the earth the seven bowls of the wrath of God.' So the first angel went and poured out his bowl on the earth, and harmful and painful sores came upon the people who bore the mark of the beast and worshiped its image" (Revelation 16:1-2 ESV)

John heard a loud voice from the temple telling the seven angels to go ahead with the work they are entrusted to do. According to the last verse (vs8) of Rev. Chapter 15 the temple was filled with smoke from the glory of God and from His power. Smoke filling the temple shows the presence of God. No one, not even the redeemed ones can enter the sanctuary in heaven during the period when these seven bowls are poured, and therefore, we can safely infer that the voice John heard from the temple was of the Lord God.

"And the temple was filled with smoke from the glory of God, and from his power; and no man was able to enter into the temple, till the seven plagues of the seven angels were fulfilled" (Revelation 15:8)

First it is the turn of the first angel to obey the command of the LORD God and he proceeds with the bowl filled with wrath of God and pours out his bowl on the earth. When the wrath of God is poured upon the earth by the first angel harmful and painful sores came upon the people who bore the "mark of the beast" and worshipped his image.

When the word of God says that the sores, which those who reject Jesus as savior, and accept Antichrist will suffer, are harmful and painful, it is beyond our imagination how intense the pain would be, and harmful those sores would be. They could be greater than the sufferings of terminally ill patients before their definite death.

The consequences of identifying with the "man of sin", who is the "son of perdition" were foretold in Revelation 14:9-11. There is no salvation for those who identify with that beast either in this age or any age to come. The "man of sin" persecutes people to worship his live image which speaks blasphemous words against God. The "man of sin" has no power over 144,000 children of Israel, who were sealed unto redemption as recorded in Revelation Chapter 7:4-8 and are seen later with the Lord on Mount Zion as recorded in Revelation Chapter 14:1.

Antichrist has power over earth-dwellers who refuse to yield to his demand of worshipping his image and refuse to take upon their foreheads or on their right hands the "mark of the beast" which is the number of man and that is 666. Those refuse to yield to his demand will become martyrs and are blessed for standing for the Lord, who will reward them according to their works.

CHAPTER 48
THE SEVEN BOWLS PART II

(From Revelation 16:1-21)

THE SEVEN BOWLS OF GOD'S WRATH

The main theme of this chapter is that God's wrath is poured upon Beast's worshippers and at the seat of Beast, the "son of perdition", who gathers kings of the earth to wage a war at "Armageddon" against the Almighty God, who conquers them and their blood is shed and stands up to a height of about four feet and to the length of 1600 furlongs, which is the distance from "Armageddon" up to the capital city of "Sela", also called "Petra" of Edom, the seat of Esau.

This is John's vision as revealed to him by Lord Jesus Christ for the benefit of us to understand the events in the last days.

The seven angels had with them the seven last plagues which were the wrath of God filled up in their bowls (cf. Rev. 15:1)

When the first angel poured out his bowl upon the earth a noisome and grievous sore fell upon the men who worshipped the image of the beast, and taken upon their forehead or on their right hand the "mark of the beast". The sores on the body depict the inward condition of one's heart and mind, evidently their heart and mind was filled with evil. They did not choose to worship the living God but chose to worship the "man of sin", who is the "son of perdition" (cf. 2 Thess.2:3; Rev. 16:2).

When the second angel poured out his bowl the sea became like the blood of a corpse, and all the sea life is killed. Imagine man's condition without the sea creatures! We depend so much on the amphibians and they are no more at this point. It is more than the ecological imbalance that would have caused due to oil spilling on sea waters by any oil company.

When the third angel poured out his bowl upon the rivers and the streams of waters, they became blood. Imagine drinking water mixed with blood and served to us! We cannot even imagine drinking water with little dirt, leave alone mixed with blood. It is so anathematic that we may have to cover our noses to prevent inhaling the foul smell emanating from it. Thus the contaminated water is no good for drinking and the irony is that Antichrist, who kills the servants of God, is served with this water mixed with blood and it is drunk by all his followers. Then the angel in charge of the waters says:

"Just are you, O Holy One, who is and who was,
        for you brought these judgments.
For they have shed the blood of saints and prophets,
and you have given them blood to drink.
It is what they deserve!"
And I heard the altar saying,
"Yes, Lord God the Almighty, true and just are your judgments!"
(Revelation 16:3-7 ESV)

When the fourth angel pours out his bowl upon the sun it receives power to scorch men with fire. Those worshippers of Antichrist, who look forward for a pleasant sunshine, are given scorching heat with fire. Imagine the condition of men who would suffer under the scorching heat that burns them with its fire.

Unable to bear the scorch with fire these worshippers of the beast blaspheme the name of God, who has power over these plagues. They suffer scorching heat from sun and eventually curse the name of God, who had the power over these plagues. It is strange that even though they suffer so much they do not repent of their sins and do not give the LORD the glory due His name.

When the fifth angel pours out his bowl filled with the wrath of God, Satan's kingdom plunges into darkness. The beast established his kingdom in the Garden of Eden, where he cheated Adam and Eve, and this is the end of it. Imagine people groping in darkness!

If shutting down power for a little while could upset our lives so much, then it deserves our pondering as to the quantum of destruction the continued presence of darkness would bring in the lives of those who choose to worship Antichrist. They, who worship this beast, gnaw their tongue in anguish and curse God of heaven for their pain and sores, and yet, surprisingly, they do not repent of their evil deeds; but enjoy living with them and in them.

When the sixth angel poured out his bowel on the great river Euphrates the waters dry out and a way is prepared for the kings of the East to come to Armageddon. (In the absence of enough land the cities are built upon the destroyed cities, which they called "Har" or "Tel", such as "Tel-Aviv" etc., and "Megiddo" is the arena where most of the battles are fought in Israel. Both words put together is called "Armageddon")

John saw three unclean demonic spirits whose appearance was like that of frogs coming out of the dragon, and out of the mouth of the beast and out the mouth of the false prophet, who constitute the Satanic Trinity. These demonic spirits performed signs, and they go abroad to the kings of the whole world to assemble for battle on the great day of God the Almighty.

The Lord comes like a thief for those who are living in darkness. Apostle Paul identifies two groups in 1 Thessalonians 5th Chapter. One group belongs to day and they are the children of light, and another belongs to the devil and they are the children of night. While the children of light are aware of the fact that the Lord will come again, His coming is surprise to those who are of the children of night.

All the kings of the world took up their cudgels to fight against the God of heavens, the Almighty God, who was, and is and is to come. Men, who are the creatures of God now, are ready to fight against the Almighty God, the creator. What an irony! It is like ants taking up arms against man.

Man cannot control even heavy downpour from heaven, or hurricanes and tornadoes, but now he takes up his sword or modern warfare to fight the Almighty God. The LORD slays all these tiny creatures that took up arms against Him and causes their blood to stand up to nearly 4 feet above the ground and up to a distance of 1600 furlongs from Armageddon unto Petra, also called Sela, which is the capital city of Edom.

When the seventh angel pours out his bowl it hits the base of Satan, who is prince of the power of the air, as Paul descries in Ephesians 2:2. As soon as the seventh bowl is poured into the air, a loud voice was heard by John and the voice that came out of the temple from the throne said "It is done".

When Jesus accomplished His mission on the cross he said "It is finished". Here the voice that came out of the temple could be of Lord Jesus Christ because the scriptures says that the Father judges no man, but has committed all judgment to the Son" (cf. John 5:22)

As the voice came out from the temple saying "It is done", there were flashes of lightning, rumblings, peals of thunder, and a great earthquake.

The great city was split into three parts, and the cities of the nations fell. God remembered Babylon the great, "to make her drain the cup of the wine of the fury of his wrath"

And every island fled away, and no mountains were to be found. And great hailstones, about one hundred pounds each, fell from heaven on people; and they cursed God for the plague of the hail, because the plague was so severe" (cf. Revelation 16:17-21)

CHAPTER 49
MYSTERY, BABYLON THE GREAT – PART I

(From Revelation 17:1-6)

THE MOTHER OF HARLOTS AND ABOMINATIONS OF THE EARTH

(The Great Prostitute and the Beast)

"And upon her forehead was a name written, MYSTERY, BABYLON THE GREAT, THE MOTHER OF HARLOTS AND ABOMINATIONS OF THE EARTH" (Revelation 17:5)

Man's rebellion against God started in the Garden of Eden. During Noah's period the wickedness increased and God punished whole world by huge deluge. In the Postdiluvian period (i.e. the period after Noah's flood), Noah's family consisting of eight members (i.e. Noah and his wife, Noah's three sons, Shem, Ham and Japheth and their wives), and the animals, fowls, and creeping creatures that were in the Ark went out of it and settled in the plains of Shinar. The ark "rested in the seventh month, on the seventeenth day of the month, upon the mountains of Ararat". (cf. Genesis 8:4)

God commanded Noah saying:

"And you, be ye fruitful, and multiply; bring forth abundantly in the earth, and multiply therein" (Genesis 9:7).

Noah cursed Ham, one of his sons, for that which he did to his father (cf. 9:22-26)

"And Noah awoke from his wine, and knew what his younger son had done unto him. And he said, Cursed be Canaan; a servant of servants shall he be unto his brethren. And he said, Blessed be the LORD God of Shem; and Canaan shall be his servant" (Genesis 9:24-26)

THE TOWER OF BABEL

Whereas God said to Noah and his family to be fruitful, multiply, and bring forth abundantly in the earth, his offspring settled in the land of "Shinar" against the will of God. It is in Shinar that the earliest form of Paganism originated. Paganism is worship of many gods, goddesses, and deities, as in ancient Greece and Rome.

Thereafter they made attempts to build for themselves a city and "a tower with its top in the heavens". God saw their reluctance to be dispersed over the face of the whole earth and the "city and the tower, which the children of man had built". The LORD said if the people are one and have one language, and this being the beginning, then nothing would prevent them doing things impossible for them.

Therefore, He confused their languages that they may not understand one another's speech and dispersed them over the face of the earth and they gave up building the city and the tower. That city was called "BABEL" (cf. Genesis 11:1-9 ESV)

"Babel" was ruled by the world's first dictator Nimrod, who was the son of Cush, son of "Ham", who was a cursed man. Nimrod began to be a mighty man in the earth who went in defiance of God and his kingdoms were Babel, Erech, Accad, and Calneh in the land of Shinar, and from this kingdoms came forth Asshur (which was later called Assyria, Nineveh (cf. Genesis 10:8-11)

According to International Standard Bible Encyclopedia "ba'-bel, bab'-i-lon (Topographical): Babylon was the Greek name of the city written in the cuneiform script of the Babylonians, bab-ili, which means in Semitic, "the gate of god." The Hebrews called the country, as well as the city, Babhel. This name they considered came from the' root, balal, "to confound" (Ge 11:9)".

Jewish historian Flavius Josephus identifies Babel as Babylon and Nimrod as the great ruler who rebelled against God.

"Now it was Nimrod who excited them to such an affront and contempt of God. He was the grandson of Ham, the son of Noah, a bold man, and of great strength of hand. *He persuaded them not to ascribe it to God, as if it were through his means they were happy, but to believe that it was their own courage which procured that happiness.* He also gradually *changed the government into tyranny*, seeing no other way of turning men from the fear of God, but to *bring them into a constant dependence on his power. He also said he would be revenged on God*, if he should have a mind to drown the world again; for that he would build a tower too high for the waters to reach. And that he would avenge himself on God for destroying their forefathers". (Ref. Flavius Josephus, Antiquities of Jews, Bk1, and Ch. 4: Page 19)

"The place wherein they built the tower is now called *Babylon,* because of the confusion of that language which they readily understood before; for the Hebrews mean by the word *Babel,* confusion" (Ref. Josephus - *"Antiquities of the Jews"* - 01 of 20; Ch.4: Concerning the Tower of Babylon, and the confusion of Tongues)

All forms of idolatry and occultist practices came from Egypt and Babylon. The angel in Revelation 14:8 declared saying "'Fallen, fallen is Babylon the great, she who made all nations drink the wine of the passion of her sexual immorality.'" (Revelation 14:8 ESV)

God revealed to Prophet Ezekiel as to how the children of Israel have stooped from worshipping the true God down to lamenting over the death of a pagan god namely Tammuz.

"The Babylonian myth represents Dumuzu, or Tammuz, as a beautiful shepherd slain by a wild boar, the symbol of winter... This mourning for Tammuz was celebrated in Babylonia by women on the 2nd day of the 4th month, which thus acquired the name of Tammuz. This custom of weeping for Tammuz is referred to in the Bible in the only passage where the name occurs (Ezekiel 8:14) – Source: H. Porter, International Standard Bible Encyclopedia, and 1st Paragraph.

People in Judah and in the streets of Jerusalem worshipped moon ("the queen of heaven and god") and provoked God to rage in anger against them. The LORD said to Jeremiah not to mediate on their behalf until He pours out His wrath on them.

The children gather wood, and the fathers kindle the fire, and the women knead their dough, to make cakes to the queen of heaven, and to pour out drink offerings unto other gods, that they may provoke me to anger (cf. Jeremiah 7:16-20)

As a consequence of seventh angel pouring out his bowl filled with the wrath of God "The great city was split into three parts, and the cities of the nations fell, and God remembered Babylon the great, to make her drain the cup of the wine of the fury of his wrath" (Revelation 16:19 ESV)

There is a great prophecy in Micah 5:5-6 according to which Messiah will protect the children of Israel from the hands of the Assyrian, who comes to destroy them. The Lord will help them, in their times of trouble, to tread upon the land of Nimrod and lay waste whole of it. This is obviously a reference to Antichrist coming during "Great Tribulation" period when the Lord will protect the children of Israel.

Revelation Chapter 17 and 18 deal with the Spiritual hypocrisy. The woman identified is not only a harlot but the mother of harlots. She is decked, as a true prostitute would, with gold and precious stones and pearls, and had a golden cup in her hand, as if to entice her customers. The cup was filled with abominations and filthiness of her fornication. She was drunk with blood of saints, and with blood of the martyrs who died for the sake of the Lord during "Great Tribulation" period. (cf. Rev. 17:4-6)

One of the seven angels, who poured out seven bowls filled with of wrath of God, talked to John in his vision, according to the command of Lord Jesus Christ, and said. "Come, I will show you the judgment of the great prostitute who is seated on many waters, with whom the kings of the earth have committed sexual immorality, and with the wine of whose sexual immorality the dwellers on earth have become drunk."

As identified in verse 15 the waters are the peoples, multitudes of nations of languages and seated on them is the whore with whom they have committed sexual immorality and are drunk on that evil. The woman was sitting on a scarlet beast which was full of blasphemous names, and it had seven heads and ten horns. The color scarlet in Scriptures represents sin.

"Come now, and let us reason together, saith the LORD: though your sins be as scarlet, they shall be as white as snow; though they be red like crimson, they shall be as wool" (Isaiah 1:18)

The scarlet beast was full of blasphemous names. It is one thing to deny Lord Jesus Christ as Savior, and it another thing to blaspheme His name. Blasphemy is very serious sin and it is not forgivable in this generation or in any generation. It is so often seen people blaspheme the name of Jesus Christ in ignorance; but if they do it conscientiously it is rest assured that they will spend their eternity in hell with the beast.

It is very important to note that the woman was riding the scarlet beast. This mystery of iniquity is already at work; however, it will be revealed as soon as the "restrainer" (Holy Spirit) stops restraining him to be revealed. (cf. 2 Thessalonians 2:7)

CHAPTER 50
MYSTERY, BABYLON THE GREAT – PART II

(From Revelation 17:7-18)

THE MOTHER OF HARLOTS AND ABOMINATIONS OF THE EARTH

(The Great Prostitute and the Beast)

When John wondered greatly in admiration after seeing the mother of harlots seated on the scarlet beast that had seven heads and ten horns, the angel questioned him, as to why he marveled. The angel offered to tell him the mysteries of the women and the beast. The woman is the mother of harlots (plural) representing several false religious systems.

The angel makes a puzzling revelation to John. He said…

"The beast that you saw was, and is not, and is about to rise from the bottomless pit and go to destruction. And the dwellers on earth whose names have not been written in the book of life from the foundation of the world will marvel to see the beast, because it was and is not and is to come" (Revelation 17:8 ESV)"

Then, he reveals the mystery that the seven heads are seven mountains on which the woman sat. They are seven kingdoms, of which five had fallen (Egypt, Babylon, Assyria, Persia and Greek), one kingdom (Rome phase I), was ruling at the time when John saw the vision, and the seventh kingdom (Rome II phase) was yet to re-emerge; however, as this kingdom re-emerges it will be in power only for a short duration.

If we closely compare with the text in Daniel 2nd Chapter, Daniel 7th Chapter and Revelation 17th Chapter it is clear that the feet of iron mixed in clay of the image that Nebuchadnezzar saw in his dream is the last Roman Empire that will arise again to power. It is the same as the little horn with two horns that Daniel saw in his vision in Daniel 7th Chapter.

Mountains represent governments (cf. Daniel 2:35; 2:45). As the history proved it to be the seven heads are seven kingdoms and they are: Egypt, Babylon, Assyria, Persia, Greek, Rome and Rome II; if the history is to be taken into account the ten horns are perhaps, ten future kings, yet to come on the world scene.

The power that ruled (Rome Phase I), and was not there when John saw the vision, will come as the eighth power (Rome Phase II) as he is from the seventh; he goes into perdition (destruction). The ten horns that he saw were the ten kings, who had not yet received their kingdom but will receive power as kings for a short while with the beast.

All these kings with one accord in unity will give their power and strength to the Antichrist, the beast. These kings make war with the Lamb (Lord Jesus Christ), and will be defeated in His hands. The Lamb will overcome them inasmuch as He is the Lord of lords, and King of kings, and they that are with Him are called chosen and faithful.

Then the angel said to John that the waters that he saw are the peoples, multitudes, nations and tongues. The whore (mother of harlots, who represent false religions) was sitting on the waters, which indicates that the harlot was controlling the people.

The Ten horns that he saw upon the beast were the ten kings who, after getting deceived by her immorality with them, will hate her and will greatly insult her by making her desolate, and naked and then eat her flesh and burn her with fire.

God is in control. He puts in their hearts the desire to harass and kill the whore in order that His will may be fulfilled. He does it so in order to give their kingdoms to the beast (the Antichrist) until the words of God are fulfilled.

John says that the woman that he saw was that great city Babylon which had power over the kings of the earth.

CHAPTER 51
THE FALL OF BABYLON PART I

(From Revelation Chapter 18:1-6)

RECOMPENSE THE HARLOT

"Reward her even as she rewarded you, and double unto her double according to her works: in the cup which she hath filled fill to her double" (Revelation 18:6)

After seven angels have poured out their bowls filled with the wrath of God John saw another angel, who had great power coming down; and as he came down the earth was filled with his glory. He cried mightily with a strong voice, saying "Babylon the great is fallen, is fallen, and is become the habitation of devils, and the hold of every foul spirit, and a cage of every unclean and hateful bird"

That was a great victory of Truth prevailing over falsehood and false religious-systems. Lord Jesus said, "...I am the way, the truth, and the life: no man cometh unto the Father, but by me" (John 14:6)

The first message of Christ's disciple Apostle Peter to the audience was that God raised Jesus from the dead; and there is no salvation in any other. He said there is no other name under heaven by which we must be saved (cf. Acts 4:10-12).

Antichrist, who could appropriately be called as "Pseudo-Christ" is that beast which came out the sea and that beast is the "man of sin" who is also called the "son of perdition". Another beast that came out the earth was the false prophet, who had the power to make the image of the first beast to speak and cause many to worship the image of the beast and those who did not worship the image of the first beast was killed.

The first beast spoke blasphemous words against God and exalted himself as god. The woman in this chapter was the mother of harlots, who was Babylon that rode on the first beast and controlled the world's false religious systems. The Kings of the world, the merchants, and captains of the ship committed fornication with her and have become pawns in the hands of that great whore.

Judgment was near and before that Pseudo-Christ and false prophet are thrown into "lake of fire" they are defeated by the Lord, and the angel testifies the victory of Truth over falsehood by proclaiming emphatically by saying:

"...Fallen, fallen is Babylon the great! She has become a dwelling place for demons, a haunt for every unclean spirit, a haunt for every unclean bird, a haunt for every unclean and detestable beast. For all nations have drunk the wine of the passion of her sexual immorality, and the kings of the earth have committed immorality with her, and the merchants of the earth have grown rich from the power of her luxurious living." (Rev. 18:2, 3)

It is twice said that Babylon the great is fallen. She became "a dwelling place for demons, a haunt for every unclean spirit, a haunt for every unclean bird, a haunt for every unclean and detestable beast".

When Jesus was on this earth he cast away the unclean spirits (evil spirits) from demon-possessed people (cf. Mark 5:13), he spoke of birds, which in scriptures are considered as evil, carried away the seed (cf. Matthew 13:4, 31), and to be careful that no man may deceive His disciples, inasmuch as many shall come deceiving many in His name, saying "I am Christ". (cf. Matthew 24:4-5)

However, the children of God are comforted greatly in the words of John, who heard another voice from heaven that said "Come out of her, my people, that ye be not partakers of her sins, and that ye receive not of her plagues".

What a great invitation to the children of God that they will not be partakers of the sins committed by the whore, the mother of harlots, which is Babylon, and that they will not be tormented with plagues.

When God takes care of His people, it is perfect and devoid of any flaw. His protection is complete and invincible. God said to Noah to take his wife and his three sons and daughters and enter into the Ark, they obeyed the LORD, and after it rained for forty days and forty nights, every living creature outside the Ark died, but the family of eight were safe and intact in the Ark and they came out as they went into the Ark; none were lost.

God undertook to seal 144,000 descendants of Israel and did what He said and protected them from the "man of sin". They were all seen with the Lord on Mount Zion. (cf. Revelation 14:1). Jesus prayed to the Father (cf. John 17:12) that all those disciples who were given by the Father to Him were kept by Him in Father's name, and none of them was lost, except the son of perdition (who was Judas Iscariot). In the loss of Judas Iscariot the scriptures were fulfilled (cf. Psalm 41:9).

Revelation18:20 is a great comforting verse that says: "Rejoice over her, thou heaven, and ye holy apostles and prophets; for

God hath avenged you on her". The heaven, holy apostles, and prophets are asked to rejoice because the mother of harlots is put to tremendous shame.

MYSTERY, BABYLON THE GREAT, THE MOTHER OF HARLOTS AND ABOMINATIONS OF THE EARTH, the great prostitute glorified herself and lived with power, as kings, merchants, and captains of the ships committed fornication with her.

The Lord gave her double the torment than that she gave to the children of God. He gave her the cup filled with double the wrath than that of her cup which she filled and gave to the children of God. The time to recompense is at hand. God revealed His plans and His judgments, and blessings through the vision given to John for our guidance, reproof and admonition.

The pleasures of the world, the false religious-systems, and the wealth of this world are all like those who stand on slippery places; a day would come when they face unbearable shame. The end is disastrous for those who seek worldly pleasures. Know the Truth, and the truth shall set you free. The Psalmist said:

"until I went into the sanctuary of God; then I discerned their end. Truly you set them in slippery places; you make them fall to ruin. How they are destroyed in a moment, swept away utterly by terrors!" Psalm 73:17-19 ESV)

CHAPTER 52
THE FALL OF BABYLON PART II

(From Revelation Chapter 18:7-14)

RECOMPENSE THE HARLOT

Babylon the great city, which is called the mother of harlots, has made all nations drunk with wine to commit sin with her. The merchants of the earth increased their wealth through the abundance of her power. The sins of Babylon reached unto heaven and God remembered her iniquities.

Not only she did sin, and made nations to sin, but she boasted herself as not a widow in comparison with the woman in Revelation chapter 12. Her boasting was because Israel committed sin by worshipping idols, and other gods, in violation to the commandment given by God, who, then said He gave a bill of divorce to her. Israel was considered as the wife of God just as the Church is considered as the bride of Lord Jesus Christ.

"And I saw, when for all the causes whereby backsliding Israel committed adultery I had put her away, and given her a bill of divorce; yet her treacherous sister Judah feared not, but went and played the harlot also" (Jeremiah 3:8)

One thing that does not come to the mind of the 'mother of harlots' is that God made an unconditional covenant with Abraham from whose loins came forth Israel. God chastises Israel but He does not forget the unconditional covenant He made with Israel that they are His people and He will bless them.

Because of the sins of Babylon the plagues that come upon her will be sudden. Kings bewail her, and lament for her, when they shall see the smoke of her burning. They see the smoke of her burning when the plagues come upon her and so quickly its destruction will be that Bible says the duration is 'one hour'. Standing afar off for the fear of her torment they say, "Alas, alas, that great city Babylon, that mighty city! for in one hour is thy judgment come". Merchants of the earth shall weep and mourn for her and no one buys their merchandise any more.

It is for avoiding any allegory of the cargo, spices and condiments that God detailed twenty eight of them such as gold, and silver, and precious stones, and of pearls, and fine linen, and purple, and silk, and scarlet, and all thyine wood, and all manner vessels of ivory, and all manner vessels of most precious wood, and of brass, and iron, and marble, and cinnamon, and odors, and ointments, and frankincense, and wine, and oil, and fine flour, and wheat, and beasts, and sheep, and horses, and chariots, and slaves, and souls of men are mentioned. They are literal and the destruction of Babylon will be literal.

God spoke His word though Prophet Jeremiah that Babylon's destruction was sure and imminent. The LORD said He will execute judgment upon her images, and every image-worshipper will be judged. Every idol-worshipper will be wounded and will groan. No matter how Babylon fortifies herself even up to the heaven; the LORD says He will send destroyers against her. Here is the voice that is heard "A voice!

A cry from Babylon! The noise of great destruction from the land of the Chaldeans! "(cf. Jeremiah 51:51-54)

The fruit that she lusted after will be gone, and all that was delicious and goodly will be gone from her and she will not find them anymore. The merchants who became rich by selling the riches of her will not only wail on her fall, but also wail on their poverty caused by the lack of business. Shipmasters who carried their cargo will cry at the fall of Babylon. All those affected by her fall will mourn and will wonder if there was any city greater than this city before.

Amidst all this fall God calls His children to rejoice over her fall because the LORD avenged them on her. A mighty angel took up a stone like a great millstone and cast it into the sea saying, "Thus with violence shall that great city Babylon be thrown down, and shall be found no more at all".

There will be no music or voice heard from harpers, musicians, pipers, and trumpeters. No craftsman shall be found anymore in her land; not even the sound of the millstone anymore because the city will never rise again.

There will be no light to shine in her land not even of a candle. There will be no more wedding or joy in her land; no more a bride or bridegroom. She will be rewarded double her iniquity for the sorceries that she performed on her merchants, who became great men in the earth.

This calls for remembrance of wicked Jezebel wife of Ahab who did much evil to the prophets of God and was killed in most ignominious way; the dogs licked her blood. Likewise, in Babylon "was found the blood of prophets, and of saints, and all that were slain upon the earth" and rightly so, the LORD will punish her to render justice.

The LORD judges every evil but to those who have received salvation through Lord Jesus Christ there will be life everlasting in plenty. It is time for the unrepentant to repent and accept Lord Jesus Christ as personal savior.

(cf. Isaiah 13:1-22; 1 Thess. 5:3; Joel 1:15; 2:10; Jeremiah 50:16; Romans 10:9-10)

CHAPTER 53
PRAISE THE LORD: HALLELUJAH

(From Revelation 19:1-10)

The Marriage of the Lamb

Revelation Chapter 19 begins with the phrase "and after these things" i.e. after the judgment of the Mystery, Babylon the great, John heard in his vision a great voice of many people saying in heaven, "Alleluia; Salvation, and glory, and honour, and power, unto the Lord our God" They continued saying true and righteous are His judgments because He judged the "mother of harlots", who did corrupt the earth with her fornication.

What a great joy it was to praise the Lord for avenging on the harlot the blood of saints killed by her. The multitudes consisting of those who have received salvation prior to "Great Tribulation", and the saints martyred during "Great Tribulation" together praise the Lord saying: "Hallelujah" several times. The twenty four elders and the four living creatures fell down and worshipped God who sat on the throne. They said "Amen; Hallelujah".

Some of those, who are in the Church age are reluctant to say "Hallelujah"; but they will all be inevitably saying "Hallelujah" to the Lord in heaven.

The joy is indescribable. The Lord recompensed the "mother of harlots" with double the wrath that she poured out on the servants of the Lord. The Lord avenged the blood of His servants. Then, again they said "Hallelujah" and the harlot's smoke rose up forever and ever signifying her total destruction never to return again similar to the destruction of Sodom and Gomorrah.

John head a voice that came out of the throne saying, "Praise our God, all ye his servants, and ye that fear him, both small and great". He continued to hear the voice as it were the voice of great multitude, and as the voice of many waters, and as the voice of mighty thunders, saying "Hallelujah" for the Lord God is omnipotent and He reigns. They saw the victory of the Lord in Revelation 17 and 18 over the beast that corrupted whole earth and the world system. They saw their prayers in Revelation 6:10.

There is an admonition to be glad and to rejoice and to give honor to Him, because the marriage of the Lamb is at hand. The Church, which is His bride, got ready for the marriage. Israel is His wife, who was unfaithful, and yet forgiven by God after chastening them. His unconditional covenant with Abraham about the children of Israel causes them to be gathered under His wings again. (cf. Genesis 12:1-3; 15:1-21; 17:7-21; Hosea 2:19-20; Isaiah 54:5)

The bride was given the privilege to be arrayed in fine linen, clean and white. The fine linen is the righteousness of saints belonging to the Church, His bride (cf. 1 Corinthians 11:2; Ephesians 5:25-32). The Church is the body of Christ as long as it is on this earth and espoused to be His wife in eternity (cf. 1 Corinthians 12:12-31; 2 Corinthians 11:2).

The Lord is waiting eagerly for the marriage and marriage supper wherein He could sup from the cup of fellowship once again with His bride.

"But I say unto you, I will not drink henceforth of this fruit of the vine, until that day when I drink it new with you in my Father's kingdom" (Matthew 26:29)

The angel said to John in the vision to write that "blessed are they which are called unto the marriage supper of the Lamb (144,000, and saints martyred during Great tribulation period). He said to John these are the true sayings of God.

John probably thought the angel who spoke to him was the Lord, or in excitement he misunderstood and fell at his feet to worship him, but he did not accept worship and said to John that he was his fellow-servant and of all the brethren who have the testimony of Jesus.

The angel admonished John to worship God because the testimony of Jesus is the spirit of prophecy. There is none, except the Lord, who should be worshipped. Only the creator deserves our worship and not any creation. Any worship of creation is idolatry and God hates idolatry.

"Then I looked, and I heard around the throne and the living creatures and the elders the voice of many angels, numbering myriads of myriads and thousands of thousands, saying with a loud voice,

"Worthy is the Lamb who was slain, to receive power and wealth and wisdom and might and honor and glory and blessing!"

And I heard every creature in heaven and on earth and under the earth and in the sea, and all that is in them, saying,

"To him who sits on the throne and to the Lamb be blessing and honor and glory and might forever and ever!"

And the four living creatures said, "Amen!" and the elders fell down and worshiped. (Revelation 5:11-14 ESV)

CHAPTER 54
THE MARRIAGE SUPPER

(From Revelation 19:11-21)

VESTURE DIPPED IN BLOOD

"And he saith unto me, Write, Blessed [are] they which are called unto the marriage supper of the Lamb. And he saith unto me, These are the true sayings of God" Revelation 19:9

"Vesture dipped in blood" has a reference to Isaiah 63:2-3 and about the trampling over the enemies of the Lord and the treading the winepress, but before that it is worth considering about the "Lamb".

The Passover Lamb was set aside on the tenth day of the first month of Jewish calendar i.e. the month of "Abib" and was slain on fourteenth day of the month (Ref. Exodus 12:1-6). The children of Israel applied the blood of the lamb to the lintel posts of the doors of their houses in order that the Lord may Passover that home without killing the first born in the house. The firstborn of the Egyptians including that of Pharaoh was killed by the Lord and then Pharaoh released the children of Israel from the bondage of slavery. "And it came to pass, that at midnight the LORD smote all the firstborn in the land of Egypt, from the firstborn of Pharaoh that sat on his throne unto the firstborn of the captive that was in the dungeon; and all the firstborn of cattle" (Exodus 12:29)

The typology of the slaying of the Lamb for the redemption of the children of Israel from the bondage of slavery is fulfilled when Lord Jesus Christ was crucified on the cross of Calvary for the redemption of mankind. Whoever believes in Jesus as Savior will have salvation free of cost and whoever rejects Him as savior will perish according to John 3:16 John the Baptist pointed to Lord Jesus Christ and identified Him as the "Lamb of God". "The next day John seeth Jesus coming unto him, and saith, Behold the Lamb of God, which taketh away the sin of the world" John 1:29

Apostle John saw in his vision as recorded in Revelation Chapter 19:13 that Lord Jesus Christ was clothed with vesture dipped in blood.

"And he [was] clothed with vesture dipped in blood: and his name is called The Word of God" Revelation 19:13 and His name was "The Word of God".

"In the beginning was the Word, and the Word was with God, and the Word was God" . (John 1:1)

The Word was made flesh and lived among us.

"And the Word was made flesh, and dwelt among us, (and we beheld his glory, the glory as of the only begotten of the Father,) full of grace and truth" (John 1:14)

Thus we see three important truths about Lord Jesus Christ.

HE IS THE LAMB OF GOD
HIS VESTURE WAS DIPPED IN BLOOD
HIS NAME IS THE WORD OF GOD

Lord Jesus Christ purchased mediatory power by shedding His own blood. He purchased the blood of His enemies over whom He prevailed by shedding His own blood. He defeated Satan at the cross and His name is the Word of God. God called things into existence. Heavens and the earth and all that is therein are created by Him. God created great whales and everything that moves in the waters. Lastly, God created man in His own image after His likeness, and gave power to him to have dominion over the fish of the sea, over the fowl of the air, over the cattle, over all the earth and every creeping thing that creeps on the earth. The LORD God did all this by His word and His word brought everything into existence. His word is double-edged sword and by His Word He will smite the nations and rule them with a rod of iron. He treads the winepress of fierceness and the wrath of Almighty God.

Lord Jesus Christ will defeat Edomites according to the prophecy in Isaiah 63:1-5. Prophet Isaiah saw the Lord coming out from Bozrah with dyed garments after trampling and treading on them all alone. The Lord is great and mighty in power in His fury He will trample over His enemies and He will have the blood of enemies sprinkled on his garments while treading the winepress all alone. It will be His day of vengeance upon them. He is righteous and mighty to save. Bozrah was a chief city in Edom where Edomites, descendants of Esau lived. Bozrah is destroyed and is no more there but the city will rise up in the end days it remains mystery now as to what the role of Bozrah would be playing in the last days.

"And he [was] clothed with vesture dipped in blood: and his name is called The Word of God" Revelation 19:13 and His name was "The Word of God".

Lord Jesus stood before Herod, who was an Edomite, a descendant of Esau, and was mocked at. Herod ridiculed Lord Jesus Christ and sent Him back to Pilate.. Pilate excused himself from rendering justice even though he knew that Lord Jesus

Christ was innocent and then all the people answered Pilate and said "…His blood be on us, and on our children" (Matthew 27:25). How could these two mortals escape from being punished for showing injustice to the Lord Jesus Christ? On the day of crucifixion of Lord Jesus Christ Herod and Pilate, who were enemies to each other became friends. The words of Jews and others inviting the curse of the blood of the Lord Jesus Christ were given unto them as gift when Titus came and destroyed Jerusalem in AD 70 and killed Jews and crucified several of them upside down on the walls of Jerusalem. But, the justice to the Edomites that includes Herod is yet future.

In reply to the question from Prophet Isaiah, the Lord says that He will tread them in His anger trampling them in His fury, and their blood shall be sprinkled upon His garments.

"Wherefore art thou red in thine apparel, and thy garments like him that treadeth in the winefat? I have trodden the winepress alone; and of the people there was none with me: for I will tread them in mine anger, and trample them in my fury; and their blood shall be sprinkled upon my garments, and I will stain all my raiment" (Isaiah 63:2-3)

The soldiers of the governor showed divine purpose in stripping Jesus and putting on Him a scarlet robe.

"And they stripped him, and put on him a scarlet robe" Matthew 27:28 The Blood of Lord Jesus Christ shed on the cross achieved multiple purposes. He defeated Satan at the cross of Calvary. He purchased us with His precious blood and we are saved not with gold or silver but in His blood by grace through faith. He purchased mediatory power and we have access to the Most Holy Place now. He purchased the power to defeat His enemies by shedding His blood on the cross and His name is the

Word of God. The armies, who are the born-again children of God will be clothed in linen, white and clean, and they follow Him from heaven and a sharp sword goes from His mouth and that word will smite the nations. He will rule the nations with rod of iron. He treads "the winepress and wrath of Almighty God" and His vesture and on His thigh a name will be seen and the name is:

"KING OF KINGS, AND LORD OF LORDS"

"And he was clothed with a vesture dipped in blood: and his name is called The Word of God. And the armies which were in heaven followed him upon white horses, clothed in fine linen, white and clean. And out of his mouth goeth a sharp sword, that with it he should smite the nations: and he shall rule them with a rod of iron: and he treadeth the winepress of the fierceness and wrath of Almighty God. And he hath on his vesture and on his thigh a name written, KING OF KINGS, AND LORD OF LORDS" (Revelation 19:13-16)

Tell the story of Redemption to the nations. It is the desire of God. "And it shall be when thy son asketh thee in time to come, saying, What is this? that thou shalt say unto him, By strength of hand the LORD brought us out from Egypt, from the house of bondage" (Exodus 13:14)

ARMAGEDDON WAR

God showed to John in visions the things that should come to pass and all prophecies about the second coming of Lord Jesus Christ will be literally fulfilled. Scriptures affirm that Heaven and earth may fail but the Lord's sayings will never fail.

"For verily I say unto you, Till heaven and earth pass, one jot or one tittle shall in no wise pass from the law, till all be fulfilled" (Matthew 5:18)

It was time for fowls of the air to be present as guests at the marriage supper, of the Lord Jesus Christ and His bride the Church, and have sumptuous meal by eating and being filled with the flesh of the enemies of the Lord.

"And he gathered them together into a place called in the Hebrew tongue Armageddon" (Revelation 16:16)

"Armageddon" is the "the mount of Megiddo", where the final battle between Lord Jesus Christ, and Antichrist and his armies, will take place. "Megiddo" is the venue for many battles that were fought as recorded in the Old Testament vide references Joshua 12:21; 17:11; Judges 1:27; 5:19; 1Kings 4:12; 9:15; 2Kings 9:27; 23:29-30; 1Chronicles 7:29; 2Chronicles 35:22.

The dragon, which is Satan, gave power to the beast, which is Antichrist. Satan deceived men to worship the beast. Men were deceived and worshipped the beast and said "Who is like unto the beast? who is able to make war with him?" . Satan gave power to Antichrist to speak blasphemy for forty two months and Antichrist opened his mouth in blasphemy against God, to blaspheme his name, and his tabernacle, and them that dwell in heaven". Antichrist was given power to wage war against the saints and to overcome them and "power was given him over all kindreds, and tongues, and nations" (Ref. Revelation 13:5-8).

After the destruction of religious Babylon by God, John heard a great voice of all the saved righteous believers praising God in heaven saying "Hallelujah: the salvation and the glory and the power of our God" (Ref. Revelation 19:1)

John heard the deafening sound, (somewhat similar to "Niagara falls"), when the servants of God said "Praise our God" and the sound was like rushing waters and thunders. They praised God loudly saying "Hallelujah, for [the] Lord our God the Almighty has taken to himself kingly power".

As the Lord Jesus Christ sat upon white horse and rode followed by His army the children of God praised again saying "Hallelujah".

"And I saw heaven opened, and behold a white horse; and he that sat upon him was called Faithful and True, and in righteousness he doth judge and make war" (Revelation 19:11)

Antichrist and the kings of the earth with their armies gathered to wage war against the Lord Jesus Christ.

The Lord's judgments are true and righteous and He "has judged the great harlot which corrupted the earth with her fornication, and has avenged the blood of his bondmen at her hand"

The redeemed saints were joyous and said to one to another encouraging rejoicing and being glad. They gave honor to the Lord because it was time for the marriage of the Lamb to take place. The Lamb is the Lord Jesus Christ (John pointed to Jesus as written in John 1:29, and said "…Behold the Lamb of God, who takes away the sin of the world").

The Church is the Lord's bride (Ref. Ephesians 5:25). She made herself ready to be united in the oncoming "Kingdom of God". God gave the bride (the Church) clean white fine linen to be arrayed in because God considered the fine linen is a sure representation of the righteousness of saints.

John saw an angel standing in the sun calling out loudly the fowl in the air flying in the midst of heaven to come and gather unto the supper of the great God that they "may eat the flesh of kings, and the flesh of captains, and the flesh of mighty men, and the flesh of horses, and of them that sit on them, and the flesh of all men, both free and bond, both small and great".

The angel said to John to write that blessed are those who were called to participate in the marriage supper of the bridegroom and the bride which was to take place on this earth. The Lord affirmed that His sayings are His true sayings, never to fail, never to be questioned, or doubted.

John fell and worshipped the angel who came to speak to him and the angel promptly said to him that he was fellow-servant of him and his brethren. The angel admonished that only God deserves worship and none else, and affirmed that the testimony of Lord Jesus was the spirit of prophecy.

As the angel continued speaking John saw heavens opening up and a white horse and He who was riding the horse. The one who sat upon the horse was called "Faithful and True, and in righteousness he doth judge and make war".

The eyes of the one who sat on the white horse were as a flame of fire and he had many crowns. He had a name written and it was not known to anyone except for Himself. His name was "The Word of God" and he was clothed with a vesture of blood indicating his victory over Satan.

The saints in heaven were as armies "clothed in fine linen, white and clean" followed the rider of the white horse from whose mouth a sharp sword went out which smote the nations. He rules the nations with rod of iron and treads "the winepress of the fierceness and wrath of Almighty God".

On the vesture of the rider of the horse was found a name written," KING OF KINGS, AND LORD OF LORDS".

The supposed great mighty battle that was to take place at Armageddon ended surprisingly with a simple word that proceeded from the Lord as John saw in his vision. It was so easy for the Lord to take Antichrist and the false prophet and cast them alive into a "lake of fire burning with brimstone".

Smoke rose up for ever and ever indicating the utter defeat of Satan. The twenty four elders representing the Church and the beasts representing the strength, wisdom, etc. fell down and worshipped saying "Amen; Hallelujah" to God who sat on the throne.

The Lord killed the remaining ones with His sword that went forth out of His mouth, and all the fowls had sumptuous marriage supper when they ate and were filled with the flesh of the enemies of the Lord.

CHAPTER 55
PEACE ON EARTH

(From Revelation Chapter 20:1-15)

The Thousand Years, Defeat of Satan, and Great White Throne Judgment

Revelation Chapter 20 deals with the thousand year reign of Lord Jesus Christ, the defeat of Satan, the judgment before the Great White Throne.

THE PROPHECY

Even before the birth of Lord Jesus Christ the angel of the Lord visited Mary and said to her that she will conceive in her womb, by the coming of the Holy Spirit on her, and by the power of Highest that shall overshadow her. Therefore, the Holy one that shall be born in her shall be called the Son of God, and His name shall be called the Son of God. The angel continued saying that "the Lord God shall give unto him the throne of David, and he shall reign over the house of Jacob for ever; and his kingdom there shall be no end" (cf. Luke 1:31-35)

The LORD made a covenant with David saying:

"I have made a covenant with my chosen, I have sworn unto David my servant, Thy seed will I establish for ever, and build up thy throne to all generations. Selah" (Psalms 89:3-4)

The LORD anointed David and said His faithfulness and mercy shall be with him. However, the LORD also said that if children forsake His law, and do not walk in his judgments, and if they break His statutes, and do not keep His commandments, then He will visit their transgression with rod. (Psalm 89:20-35)

David's son Solomon sat on his father's throne. Solomon built the temple and the LORD answered his prayer and said if Solomon walked in the ways of the LORD just as David walked, and did according to all that He commanded, then He will establish the throne of his kingdom according as He had covenanted with David; bur if turned away and forsook the LORD's statues and commandments and worshipped other gods, then He will pluck them by the roots out of His land and cast away and make a proverb and a byword among all nations. (cf. 7:16-22)

Quoting Jeremiah 25:22 some believe that Solomon's dynasty through Zedekiah continued through his daughter "Tamar Tephi" and the scepter of Judah was carried to Ireland and thus British kingdom continued through kings and queens of England. However, this view is nothing but a legend and based on many conjectures. It is quite untenable; the first reason being absence of those details in the Bible; neither did Jewish Historian Josephus give any details about this view. One author quotes and another; and another quotes yet another and none the original source. According to legend the scepter of Judah was carried through Tamar Tephi who married prince (Eochaid I (Heremon) King of Ireland, son of King Milesius and Scota) and thus David's dynasty was purportedly established. Debates on the credibility of Tama Tephi (Tamar Tephi), Tea Tephi, Teia Tephi are endless and I take them as unbelievable stories.

"And all the kings of Tyrus, and all the kings of Zidon, and the kings of the isles which are beyond the sea" (Jeremiah 25:22)

This view contradicts the reality that has happened when God chastised Solomon for his failure to keep His commandments and statues and consequently his kingdom was divided into two, and finally the "House of Israel" was scattered beyond any recognition after king Hoshea, and "House of Judah" ended up in Babylonian captivity for seventy years.

From the time Nebuchadnezzar, king of Babylon took over Jerusalem, it was the time of Gentiles, which was followed in succession by Medo-Persian Empire, Grecian Empire, and Roman Empire. It was during Roman Empire that Jesus was born.

Jesus grew up and after His baptism in Jordan River He returned to Galilee in the power of the Spirit. He taught in the synagogues of Jews, and as He came to Nazareth, where He was brought up, and as His custom was, He went to synagogue on the Sabbath day and stood up to read the word of God. He opened the Book of Isaiah and found the portion where it was written about him as...

"The Spirit of the Lord GOD is upon me; because the LORD hath anointed me to preach good tidings unto the meek; he hath sent me to bind up the brokenhearted, to proclaim liberty to the captives, and the opening of the prison to them that are bound; To proclaim the acceptable year of the LORD, and the day of vengeance of our God; to comfort all that mourn; To appoint unto them that mourn in Zion, to give unto them beauty for ashes, the oil of joy for mourning, the garment of praise for the spirit of heaviness; that they might be called trees of righteousness, the planting of the LORD, that he might be glorified" (Isaiah 61:1-3) .

However, the Lord did not read the full portion of the prophecy; but He stopped at a comma and closed the book. The phrase before the comma was:

"To proclaim the acceptable year of the LORD"

The portion after the comma was "and the day of vengeance of our God; to comfort all that mourn; To appoint unto them that mourn in Zion, to give unto them beauty for ashes, the oil of joy for mourning, the garment of praise for the spirit of heaviness; that they might be called trees of righteousness, the planting of the LORD, that he might be glorified".

Lord Jesus did it on purpose because His first mission was only up to crucifixion. His mission ended at the phrase "To proclaim the acceptable year of the LORD". The second portion of that prophecy was to be completed on His second coming, and therefore He did not read the portion:

"And he began to say unto them, This day is this scripture fulfilled in your ears" and sat down. (cf. Luke 4:14-21).

In the life time of Jesus on this earth He did not establish David's throne nor was He on the throne either physically or spiritually. He was divine and He was human who relinquished all His glory that He had in heaven and came down to fulfill the Father's desire.

When it was time it pleased the Father to bruise the Son in order that we become righteous by accepting Him as the Lord. Jesus obeyed Father's will and humbled Himself even to the point of dying on the cross; but The Father raised Him from the death and He was taken up in to heaven. He is coming back again and when He comes back He will establish David's throne and sit on it and reign for thousand years.

THE THOUSAND YEARS

The second portion of the prophecy will be fulfilled when Jesus comes again and then the scepter of the Lion of Judah will not depart from the Kingdom which will be forever and ever.

This is the second portion of the prophecy... "and the day of vengeance of our God; to comfort all that mourn; To appoint unto them that mourn in Zion, to give unto them beauty for ashes, the oil of joy for mourning, the garment of praise for the spirit of heaviness; that they might be called trees of righteousness, the planting of the LORD, that he might be glorified" (Isaiah 61:1-3).

John saw in his vision an angel who came down from heaven with the key to the bottomless pit, and a great chain. The angel seized the dragon, which is also called the serpent or Satan, or devil and bound him for a thousand years, and threw him into the bottomless pit.

One can only imagine how dark the bottomless pit would be and how much he would suffer for one thousand years with no power to play an evil or tempt anyone or deceive anyone. Satan will be bound in chains and spend the thousand years in the bottomless pit, which is shut and sealed by the angel over him.

While the devil is in bottomless pit for one thousand years, the people of God are safe and enjoy peaceful life in the kingdom, under the righteous judge and King of kings, Lord of lords, who is our Lord Jesus Christ.

John saw then thrones and on them were seated those to whom the authority to judge was given. He also saw the souls of those who bore the testimony of Jesus, and for the word of God, and became martyrs for Him during the "Great Tribulation" period. Those who did not receive the "mark of the beast" which is 666 on their forehead or on their right hands, and had not worshipped the beast, which was Antichrist (may also be called as "Pseudo-Christ") were also there.

All of them came to life and reigned with Lord Jesus Christ for a thousand years. This is the first resurrection and all those who are part of the first resurrection are blessed. There is no power for the 'death' to overcome them anymore; and they will be priests of God and of Christ.

There is condemnation and judgment for all those who are part of the second resurrection, which occurs before the end of the world; and everyone will stand before "great white throne", and be judged and thrown into 'lake of fire', which never gets extinguished.

THE DEFEAT OF SATAN

As the Lord is righteous judge He will give chance for the devil to be released from the prison at the end of the thousand year reign of Lord Jesus Christ. The devil would then go out to deceive the nations that are at the four corners of the earth, God and Magog to gather them for battle. Their number would be like that of the sand of the sea. They march up over the broad plain of the earth and surround the camp of saints and the beloved city, which is Jerusalem. However, God sends from heaven down to earth the fire that consumes them.

That is the end of the devil and he will be thrown into the "lake of fire and sulfur" where the beast (Antichrist) and the false prophet were already thrown into it before the devil was thrown. They were thrown into the 'lake of fire' when the Lord captured them before He tread the earth like treading the winepress and He came out with blood on His vesture as if it was dipped in it. The devil, the beast and the false prophet will be in the 'lake of fire' suffering torment day and night forever and ever.

Great White Throne

John saw those who refused to accept Lord Jesus Christ as their Savior standing before the "great white throne". They were all those who did not rise to life in the first resurrection. They were there to be judged. They were all rebels who refused to confess Jesus as Lord, and did not believe that God raised Him from the dead, and therefore, they were part of the second resurrection. On the "great white throne" was seated the Lord Jesus Christ, to whom was all the power to judge was given by the Father.

There was no place found for earth and sky before the Lord and they fled away. No one could hide behind any mountain or valley. All the dead, great and small were standing before the throne and then the books were opened. Then another book, which was the "book of life", was opened. All the dead were judged by what was written in the books, according to what they had done.

The sea vomited the dead who were in it. Death and Hades gave up the dead who were in them. Every one of them was judged according to what they had done. The Death and Hades were thrown into the "lake of fire" and this was the second death, which is the "lake of fire". "The book of life" is very important one, and everyone whose name was not found in the "book of life", was thrown into the "lake of fire".

The "lake of fire" is place of fire and sulfur, which keeps burning day and night, where Antichrist and False prophet were thrown first, and then the devil, followed by those whose names were not found in the "book of life". It is a place where there is torment day and night forever and ever.

Blessed are those who do not end their souls in the "lake of fire"; but be with the Lord forever and ever conformed to His image reigning with Him for thousand years, and to be as priests and Kings for God and Christ.

Now is the time to repent of sins and accept Lord Jesus Christ as personal savior. There is great blessing and peace in His kingdom. There is no sorrow nor pain nor death.

CHAPTER 56
THE ETERNITY

(From Revelation 21:1-27)

NEW HEAVEN AND NEW EARTH

CURIOSITY

Man has an unflinching curiosity to know about the power of death, the death, and the life after death. There are many myths about the death and even among Christians there are differing views. Bible gives a believer in Christ great comfort that he or she will be with the Lord for ever and ever after death.

The life after death is extremely pleasant and good according to Scriptures and, therefore, a believer in Christ does not need to be afraid of death. Lord Jesus Christ defeated the power of death, and the death once and for all, by His own resurrection.

The grave could not hold him and He resurrected without seeing any corruption of His body. Jesus said He had the power to lay down His life and take it back at his own discretion and He did so. Lord Jesus Christ also assured his followers that they need not be afraid of death because He gives them everlasting life.

According to Bible Lord Jesus Christ is the only one who has the authority to pardon sins of a person, and salvation is by grace through faith in Him. Jesus is the Son of God, and the very God Himself. Jesus became one like us and came to this earth, lived like a man among us. Jesus was fully divine and fully human and this truth is very hard to understand by an unbeliever.

Jesus died, rose on the third day and ascended into heaven. He is seated at the right hand of the Father highly exalted. He is given the name above all names and every knee shall bow to Him. Jesus will come again soon.

THE POWER OF DEATH

God commanded the man saying to him that he may freely eat of every tree of the garden but shall not eat of the tree of the knowledge of good and evil. The wages of transgression of God's command was that he shall surely die in the day he eats thereof (Genesis 2:16-17).

God made woman out of one of the ribs of man and she became man's wife. Adam and Eve lived happily until sin entered their lives through the deception by serpent who enticed Eve to eat from the forbidden tree. She not only ate the fruit from the forbidden tree but she gave it to man also and thus they became enemies to God.

Later God visited them and pronounced punishments on Serpent, Adam and Eve. Serpent was cursed and the ground was cursed for man and God said that woman will bear children in pain. God clothed Adam and Eve with coats of skin signifying that God made a way for their reconciliation (Genesis 3:1-21).

It was when Adam and Eve sinned that Satan gained power over death and death remained in his domain. It is evident from the words of Jesus that Satan has his own kingdom and demons are as his followers. (Cf. Matthew 12:24-27)

THE PROPHECIES

"For behold, I create new heavens and a new earth, and the former things shall not be remembered or come into mind" (Isaiah 65:17 ESV)

"Truly, I say to you, this generation will not pass away until all these things take place. Heaven and earth will pass away, but my words will not pass away" (Matthew 24:34-35 ESV)

"But the day of the Lord will come as a thief in the night; in the which the heavens shall pass away with a great noise, and the elements shall melt with fervent heat, the earth also and the works that are therein shall be burned up" (2 Peter 3:10)

"Then I saw a new heaven and a new earth, for the first heaven and the first earth had passed away, and the sea was no more" (Revelation 21:1 ESV)

According to the first verse in Revelation 21 John in his vision saw a new heaven and a new earth; and this was just as prophesied in Isaiah 65:17

THE NEW JERUSALEM

One of the seven angels, who had the seven bowls full of the seven last plagues, spoke to John and said to him to go the place where he would show the Bride (the Church), the wife of the Lamb (Lord Jesus Christ), and carried him away in the Spirit to a great, high mountain, and showed the holy city Jerusalem with the glory of God, coming down out of heaven from God.

The radiance of the holy city Jerusalem that John saw was like a most rare jewel namely "Jasper", which was clear as crystal. Its structure was great, often drawn by artists in different ways according to their perception.

However, according to the text it has a great high wall with twelve gates. There are twelve angels at the twelve gates. On the gates were written the names of twelves tribes of the sons of Israel. On the east there three gates, on the north three gats, on the south three gates, and on the west three gates. The wall of the city had twelve foundations. On the foundations were written the twelve names of the twelve apostles of Lord Jesus Christ.

The one who spoke to John had a measuring rod of gold with which he measured the city, its gates and its walls. The city lay foursquare; its length was the same as its breadth. The measurement of the city recorded was 12,000 furlongs i.e. about 1380 miles/1500 roman miles. The length was as much as its height i.e. they were equal in measurement. Its wall was 144 cubits (one cubit is equivalent to about 18 inches), by human measurement and by angel's as well.

STREET OF GOLD

"And the twelve gates were twelve pearls, each of the gates made of a single pearl, and the street of the city was pure gold, like transparent glass" (Revelation 21:21 ESV)

Gold is so precious in the lives of many. Imagine the joy of common people, who cannot afford to possess it; but were saved by the blood of Lord Jesus Christ. They will tread gold under their feet and walk on it in heaven. There is that street of gold in the holy city Jerusalem where those whose sins are cleansed, by the precious blood of Lord Jesus Christ, will walk on the street of gold.

John saw the Holy city, which is New Jerusalem, "coming down out of heaven from God prepared as a bride adorned for her husband. And I heard a loud voice from the throne saying, 'Behold, the dwelling place of God is with man. He will dwell with them, and they will be his people, and God himself will be with them as their God. He will wipe away every tear from their eyes, and death shall be no more, neither shall there be mourning, nor crying, nor pain anymore, for the former things have passed away.'" (Revelation 21:2-4 ESV)

The description is the holy city Jerusalem is great. Who is this bride? Bible speaks of the bride as the Church/Assembly constituting the believers in Christ, the saved ones. The bride is adorned waiting for her husband to come and here is the chaste virgin, adorned waiting for the New Jerusalem.

The tabernacle is referred to in the Old Testament, as the sacred tent into which God came and dwelt. Here in this chapter John saw God himself coming down and dwelling among his people, who will be his people, and He will be their God. The Lord will wipe away all their tears, and there will be no more death, nor sorrow, nor crying, no more pain, because all the old things have passed away by then.

God told us through His servants about the life of the saved souls in eternity where there will be great joy and rest. The prophecies and the hope that we have about the future comfort us. Our life in future will not be wasted away in darkness in the fiery furnace, which keeps burning with sulfur where the torment never ceases.

Nothing that is unclean will ever enter into the holy city Jerusalem; nor will those whose names are not found the "book of life" will enter therein.

It surprises us when we read that there is no sea in eternity. True, the sea has always been an obstruction in man's life; it retards transportation, communication, and retards progress. Therefore, it is a blessing that there is no sea in eternity.

But one of the soldiers with a spear pierced his side, and forthwith came there out blood and water. (John 19:34)

Lord Jesus Christ suffered not only pain when he was beaten; but He was mocked when He was crowned with a 'crown of thorns'. When the one of the soldiers pierced His side with his spear blood and water came forth; and it is by that blood that we are saved. He suffered on the cross of Calvary in order that we confess Him as Lord and receive salvation. Our sin is cleansed and we are made clear as crystal.

The New Jerusalem, where we will live, does not need sun and moon to shine in it because the glory of God that shines in it is greater than any light. The Lamb of God, who is our Lord Jesus Christ, is the light in it.

"And the city has no need of sun or moon to shine on it, for the glory of God gives it light, and its lamp is the Lamb" (Revelation 21:23 ESV)

"But as for the cowardly, the faithless, the detestable, as for murderers, the sexually immoral, sorcerers, idolaters, and all liars, their portion will be in the lake that burns with fire and sulfur, which is the second death." (Revelation 21:8 ESV)

In the beginning God called light into existence. He saw that the light was good and divided the light from darkness (cf. Genesis1:4-5)

On the fourth day of creation God made two great lights - the greater to rule the day and the lesser to rule the night and He made stars also. We know them by 'sun' and 'moon'. God set them in "firmament of the heaven to divide the day from the night; and let them be for signs, and for seasons, and for days, and years".

All things of old will be uncreated and destroyed. The One who is seated on the throne said "Behold I am making all things new" and said to John to write down that His words are trustworthy and true. He said to John "It is done! I am the Alpha and Omega, the beginning and the end.

He promised to give the springs of water of life free of cost to the one who is thirsty. The one who secures victory over evil will have the heritage promised by Him; and the LORD will be His God and he will be His son.

The portion allotted to all those who are cowardly, the faithless, the hateful, as for murderers, the sexual perverted, sorcerers, idolaters, and all liars, is the torment in the "lake of fire" with fire and sulfur, which burns forever and ever. Their life in the "lake of fire" is called the "second death".

The wall was built by jasper; the city was by pure gold; like a clear glass. The foundations of the city wall were decked with every kind of Jewel. The precious elements with which the city was built were, "jasper, the second sapphire, the third gate, the fourth emerald, the fifth onyx, the sixth carnelian, the seventh chrysolite, the eighth beryl, the ninth topaz, the tenth chrysoprase, the eleventh jacinth, the twelfth amethyst".

"And the twelve gates were twelve pearls, each of the gates made of a single pearl, and the street of the city was pure gold, like transparent glass"

John did not see temple in the city because its temple was the Lord God Almighty and Lord Jesus Christ. The city did not have sun or moon to shine on it because the glory of God gave it light, and its lamp was the Lord Jesus Christ.

The nations walked by the light of the glory of God and by Lord Jesus Christ, who was the lamp of the city. The gates of the city will never close by day and there was no night there. The nations bring into the city the glory and honor of the nations.

Except for those whose names are written in the Lamb's "book of life", none will enter into it, and no one who is detestable or false will enter into the city.

It is time for those, who have not accepted Jesus Christ as their Messiah, to understand this truth, and repent of their sins. Confess Jesus is the Lord, and believe in heart that God raised Him from the dead, and receive everlasting life in eternity. His name along may be glorified. Hallelujah. Amen

CHAPTER 57
FINAL WORDS

(Revelation 22:1-21)

THE RIVER OF LIFE

The angel showed to John the river of water of life, which was bright as crystal and it flowed from the throne of God, and of Lord Jesus Christ through the middle of the street of the holy city New Jerusalem.

The moment we hear that there will be no sea in eternity, it surprises us and we tend to think that there will be no water in eternity; but it is not so. There is plenty of water; not just the water but the water of life.

Both absence of sea in the New Jerusalem, and the presence of river therein are blessing to the saved. Old Testament uses the pictures of river as also of water many-a-time to depict the blessings of the Lord. However, the rivers about which the scriptures mentions are neither allegorical nor symbolical but are real.

There went out of Garden of Eden to water the garden a river which parted into four heads; the first one was Psion, Second River was Gihon, the third river was Hiddekel, and the fourth was river Euphrates. There went up mist from the earth and watered the whole face of the ground; obviously it did not rain in the beginning. Man and woman lived in this wonderful garden.

Each river encompassed certain portion of land. Unique among was Pison, which encompassed the whole land of Havilah, where gold of good quality was found. It also had precious stones viz. bdellium and the onyx stone.

Man's disobedience and transgression of God's commandment caused the ground to be cursed by God, and the Garden of Eden was once for fall shut for them.

If only the woman transgressed and man not participated in her actions, perhaps woman would have been lost eternally; however, man ate of the forbidden fruit knowing pretty well the consequences such transgression would bring. Innocent man became sin for the sake of woman and the man is called the "first Adam".

"For Adam was first formed, then Eve. And Adam was not deceived, but the woman being deceived was in the transgression. Notwithstanding she shall be saved in childbearing, if they continue in faith and charity and holiness with sobriety" (1 Timothy 2:13-15).

When Adam and Eve sinned then there arose the necessity of their redemption and shadow of covering their sin and forgiveness is indicated in the first act of God when he covered their naked bodies with the skin of an animal, obviously by shedding its blood.

"Unto Adam also and to his wife did the LORD God make coats of skins, and clothed them" (Genesis 3:21)

The redemption plan that started in the Garden of Eden continued through ages in different ways to finally culminate in the crucifixion of Jesus on the cross. He died for our sake, was buried and rose from the dead, and after forty days on this earth in His resurrected body appearing to many and leaving behind infallible proofs, He ascended into heaven. He is coming again; and we wish, just as John wished, "Amen. Come, Lord Jesus!"

It was picturesque presentation of rivers in some references to depict the richness, provision and peace, such as the peace that man had by following the LORD's commandments; it was as a river.

"And it shall be in that day, that living waters shall go out from Jerusalem; half of them toward the former sea, and half of them toward the hinder sea: in summer and in winter shall it be" (Zechariah 14:8)

A preview of blessings in the New Heavens and the new earth is presented to us in the millennial period by Ezekiel the prophet.

"Then said he unto me, These waters issue out toward the east country, and go down into the desert, and go into the sea: which being brought forth into the sea, the waters shall be healed" (Ezekiel 47:8)

There shall be River of life during the millennial period when the waters flow from four sides of Ezekiel Temple, grow deeper and wider until they reach a level when man can swim in them.

On the bank of the river there will grow many trees on its either side for meat, and the leaf of those trees "shall not fade, neither shall the fruit thereof be consumed: it shall bring forth new fruit according to his months, because their waters they issued out of the sanctuary: and the fruit thereof shall be for meat, and the leaf thereof for medicine".

The water flows to the eastern region and "goes down into the Arabah, and enters the sea; when the water flows into the sea, the water will become fresh" (cf. Ezekiel 47:1-7, 8, 9-12)

Here, a notable point is that the river water flows into the sea (the sea mentioned here is "Dead Sea"), and according to Revelation 21:1 there will be no more sea in eternity, corroborating to the view that Ezekiel's temple and the river mentioned there, pertain to millennial period.

The blessings in the New Heavens and the new earth are far greater than the ones in millennial period. Comfort, peace, richness and provision are found in the new heavens and the New Earth.

On either side of the river in the midst of the street of the New Jerusalem, which is the bride of Christ, there was seen by John the tree of life, which bore twelve kinds of fruit, and yielded her fruit every month. Eat the fruit if you wish to or do not if you do not have to.

There shall be no curse. The curse is all gone; and there is nothing but blessing, peace and rest. Worship the Lord in the beauty of His holiness.

The leaves of the tree were for the healing of the nations. The throne of God and of Lord Jesus Christ shall be in New Jerusalem. His servants shall serve Him. They will see His face and His name will be on their foreheads.

They are conformed to the image of Lord Jesus Christ and the mark on their foreheads is their identity that they belong to the God who lives forever and ever. There will be no more night. They need no light of a lamp or sun because the Lord God will be their light, and they will reign forever and ever. (cf. Revelation 22:2-5)

JESUS IS COMING

The blessings in eternity are too many to comprehend fully by mortals like us, who have lived all our life on this cursed earth. That is the reason why the angel says to John that the words written here are trustworthy and true. Angel emphasizes that "the Lord, the God of the spirits of the prophets, has sent his angel to show his servants what must soon take place."

"And behold, I am coming soon. Blessed is the one who keeps the words of the prophecy of this book."

Johns testifies that he is the one who heard and saw all that is mentioned in this book and when he heard and saw them, he fell down to worship at the feet of the angel who showed to him.

As John was about to worship the angel, he said to John that he should not worship him; because he was a fellow servant with him, and of his brothers and prophets, and with those who keep the words of this book. He, then, admonished John to worship God.

While Daniel was advised to seal up the things that will come during the last days (cf. Daniel 12:4), John was admonished here in this book not to seal up the words of the prophecy of this book; but to keep them open, which indicates that the last days of this heaven and earth are imminent.

The angel said to John that "the time is near. Let the evildoer still do evil, and the filthy still be filthy, and the righteous still do right, and the holy still be holy."

Lord Jesus Christ said:

"Behold, I am coming soon, bringing my recompense with me, to repay each one for what he has done. I am the Alpha and the Omega, the first and the last, the beginning and the end."

"Blessed are those who wash their robes, so that they may have the right to the tree of life and that they may enter the city by the gates. Outside are the dogs and sorcerers and the sexually immoral and murderers and idolaters, and everyone who loves and practices falsehood"

"I, Jesus, have sent my angel to testify to you about these things for the churches. I am the root and the descendant of David, the bright morning star."

"The Spirit and the Bride say, "Come." And let the one who hears say, "Come." And let the one who is thirsty come; let the one who desires take the water of life without price"

"I warn everyone who hears the words of the prophecy of this book: if anyone adds to them, God will add to him the plagues described in this book, and if anyone takes away from the words of the book of this prophecy, God will take away his share in the tree of life and in the holy city, which are described in this book"

"He who testifies to these things says, "Surely I am coming soon." Amen. Come, Lord Jesus!"

"The grace of the Lord Jesus be with all. Amen"

AUTHOR'S NOTE

As we meditate and understand the Book of Revelation, I pray to God that He would forgive me, if I have inadvertently added and removed any word from the word of God. It was and is my sincere effort to understand and explain the Book of Revelation to the best of my knowledge. My explanation of the Book of Revelation should be considered as only as an aide to understand the text in the Bible, and it is not a replacement or an alternative to the text in the said Book.

My prayer is that every reader should read the text in the Book of Revelation as is presented in the Bible, and understand that which is written in it, with the help of Holy Spirit.

SOME ARGUMENTS FROM AUTHOR

If the scripture says the heavenly bodies will be burned up and dissolved, then it is what it is; and it is as the text says. It does not say anything about renovation.

"But the day of the Lord will come like a thief, and then the heavens will pass away with a roar, and the heavenly bodies will be burned up and dissolved, and the earth and the works that are done on it will be exposed.

Since all these things are thus to be dissolved, what sort of people ought you to be in lives of holiness and godliness, waiting for and hastening the coming of the day of God, because of which the heavens will be set on fire and dissolved, and the heavenly bodies will melt as they burn!" (2 Peter 3:10-12 ESV)

If the Scripture says a new heaven and a new earth, for the first heaven and the first earth had passed away, then it is what it is; and it is as the text says. It does not say anything about renovation.

"Then I saw a new heaven and a new earth, for the first heaven and the first earth had passed away, and the sea was no more" (Revelation 21:1 ESV)

If the prophecy says that God will create new heavens and a new earth, and the former shall not be remembered or come into mind, then it is what it is; and it is as the text says. It does not say anything about renovation.

"For behold, I create new heavens and a new earth, and the former things shall not be remembered or come into mind. (Isaiah 65:17 ESV)

The church is identified as the bride of Christ and if the text says the holy city New Jerusalem is "coming down out of heaven from God, prepared as a bride adorned for her husband", then it is; and it is as the text says; and not for Israel (cf.Eph.5:25-27; 2 Cor. 11:2; Rev. 21:2).

The division of the land in Israel for the twelve tribes of Israel is detailed in Ezekiel Chapter 47:13-24; 48:1-36.

INVITATION TO SALVATION

With the blessings recorded in the Book of Revelation, I wonder how reader could miss to possess them. It is high time for the one who has not known the love of God in Christ, and not repented of sins yet; my prayer is that one should immediately believe that Jesus is the Lord and God raised Him from the dead. He lives forever and ever. He is coming soon!

John wrote by the will of God as:

"He who testifies to these things says, "Surely I am coming soon." Amen. Come, Lord Jesus! The grace of the Lord Jesus be with all. Amen. (Revelation 22:20-21 ESV)

"Amen. Even so, come, Lord Jesus. The grace of our Lord Jesus Christ be with you all. Amen" (Revelation 22:20b-21)